ST SYMEON THE NEW THEOLOGIAN
ON THE MYSTICAL LIFE
vol . 1: The Church and the Last Things

St Symeon the New Theologian
ON THE MYSTICAL LIFE: THE ETHICAL DISCOURSES

vol. 1: *The Church and the Last Things*
(ISBN 0-88141-142-6)

vol. 2: *On Virtue and Christian Life*
(ISBN 0-88141-143-4)

vol. 3: *Life, Times and Theology*
(ISBN 0-88141-144-2)

St Symeon The New Theologian
ON THE MYSTICAL LIFE: THE ETHICAL DISCOURSES
Vol. 1: The Church and the Last Things

Translated from the Greek and introduced

by

ALEXANDER GOLITZIN

ST. VLADIMIR'S SEMINARY PRESS
CRESTWOOD, NY 10707-1699
1995

The benefactors who have made this publication possible
wish to dedicate it in thanksgiving for their children,
Michael, David, King and Olivia.

Library of Congress Cataloging-in-Publication Data

Symeon, the New Theologian, Saint, 949-1022
    On the mystical life: the ethical discourses / St. Symeon, the New
Theologian; translated from the Greek and introduced by Alexander
Golitzin.
        p.   cm.
    Includes bibliographical references and indexes.
    Contents: vol. 1 (alk. paper)
        1. Spiritual life—Orthodox Eastern Church—Early works to 1800.
2. Monastic and religious life—Early works to 1800. 3. Mysticism—
Orthodox Eastern Church—Early works to 1800. 4. Orthodox Eastern
Church—Doctrines—Early works to 1800.   I. Golitzin, Alexander.
II. Title.
BX382.S96   1995
248.4'819—dc20
                                                    95-36925
                                                    CIP

ISBN 0–88141–142–6

PRINTED IN THE UNITED STATES OF AMERICA

Contents

The *Ethical Discourses*:
Date, Type, and Content

With this publication we present to the American reader the last significant body of work by St Symeon, eleventh-century abbot of the monastery of St Mamas in Constantinople and called the New Theologian, to await translation into English. The late C.J. de Catanzaro, George Maloney, and Paul McGuckin, respectively, have already provided English translations of St Symeon's *Catechetical Discourses*, his *Hymns of Divine Love*, the *Theological Chapters* and the *Three Theological Discourses* (for the listing, see our bibliography below). Together with the present work, and in the interests of completing the body of the saint's work available in English, we have appended the text of his *Letter on Confession* (in volume three of the present work, forthcoming). We hope that the availability of his works will encourage and speed their reading by specialists and nonspecialists, clergy and laity, both within the Orthodox Church and beyond.

A wide readership is surely what the saint himself would have desired. Although he spoke and wrote for an audience comprised chiefly of monks, St Symeon nonetheless felt his message to be applicable to all Christians, to everyone seeking an encounter with the risen Lord, Jesus Christ. The Discourses translated here contain some of his most powerful writing on the nature of that encounter. They are at once personal, yet rooted at the same time in the objective fact of the Word Who became flesh for our sake, and in Whose risen body, the Church, we are to find the reality—even in this life—of the world to come, the new Jerusalem, whose light is "the glory of God" and whose "lamp is the lamb."[1] This is, of course, nothing new. St Symeon's is the same message as that of the Gospels, the writings of St Paul, and of all the fathers and mothers of the Church "who in every age have been wellpleasing to God." At the same time, however, there are aspects of this saint and his message, particularly we might say in his "delivery," which are unique in ways that allow him to speak as directly to the reader in late twentieth-century America as he did to his audience in early eleventh-century Byzantium.

The *Ethical Discourses* appear to reflect the atmosphere of controversy surrounding St Symeon during the first decade of the eleventh century, in particular from 1003 to 1009.[2] With the exception of the concluding four discourses (numbers 11-15), and the VIIIth on the love of God, every one of the ten remaining— and far and away longer and more extensive—treatises include one or more sections devoted specifically to the castigation of his opponents, usually in very sharp language. The opposition, however, is never named. We would have been quite ignorant even of the name of Stephen of Nicomedia had not Nicetas[3] dwelt at length on him in the *Life*. Symeon never mentions him, save for the address heading *Hymn* 22: "to Stephen, a monk." The chancellor does not appear anywhere by name in the discourses printed below, nor does anyone else. Thus, while Symeon addresses his opposition directly with some frequency, as in the concluding section of the first discourse and the opening of the second, or the dialogue in Discourse V, the lack of names contributes to something of a generalized impression of his opponents. Similarly, while in other discourses, such as VII, he states that he is address-

1 Rev 21:33.
2 Darrouzès, *SC* 122, 9-10. For complete bibliographical references see our Introduction in volume III, forthcoming.
3 For the story of Stephen of Nicomedia's struggle with Symeon, and Nicetas Stethatos' *Life* of the saint, see our Introduction, Part I, in volume III of this work, forthcoming.

ing monks, it is not clear whether or not he is speaking to the monastic order in general, or to a specific community such as his own. Likewise, the reader will come across sections apparently directed to someone in particular, "your Charity,"[4] but the interlocutor is never named or otherwise identified. Neither do these treatises as a whole ever seem to carry the same sense of intimacy with others, the recollection of particular details in a community's life or the response to specific events, that one finds so abundantly in Symeon's *Catecheses*. The conclusion must be that the *Ethical Discourses* were never intended as "discourses" *per se*, i.e., as speeches or letters directed to any one particular recipient or group. The interlocutors function rather as a literary device. These works thus comprise Symeon's formal justification of his position regarding the spiritual life and the systematic reproof of his detractors as a generalized group. In addition, although Nicetas mentions the "ethical discourses" together with another collection of writings, the "apologetic and antirrhetic" treatises,[5] it seems to us that the latter answer practically as well as the former to the contents of the works translated below. The latter do indeed deal with the Christian virtues, are thus "ethical," but in so doing they also strive both to explain the New Theologian's characteristic emphases and assertions regarding both himself and his spiritual father, and to demonstrate why his enemies are in the wrong. If this is so, then the dating of these works suggested in the opening line of this paragraph might have to be revised, particularly in light of Nicetas' statement elsewhere in the *Life* that the saint composed "powerful replies" to his opponents during the last period of his life,[6] that is, during his voluntary exile on the far side of the Bosphorus (ca. 1010-1022).

Whatever the question of dating, it is indisputable that the

---

4 Eg., *ED* IV, 241-2.

5 *Vie* 134 (197).

6 Ibid. 111 (155).

Ethical Discourses are the work of Symeon's mature thought. In saying that, and in using the word "systematic" above, we do not mean to suggest that they are the work of what is called today a "systematic theologian," i.e., one who proceeds on the basis of philosophy to elucidate the data of the Christian faith. Not to put too fine a point on it, such an approach was anathema to the New Theologian. His anger is never so fierce as when he is directing it against bookish theologians, people whom he tends to lump to-gether with spiritual "quacks," and whom he sees as pretending to a knowledge they do not have, a peculiarly vile act because in so doing they lead both themselves and others astray. He is not a formal theologian, nor certainly does he have the intellectual subtlety and consistency of a Gregory of Nyssa or a Maximus Confessor;[7] but, that being said, it would also be quite untrue to characterize him—as his disciple, Nicetas, loves to do in order to prove that his master was "taught by God (*theodidaktos*)"[8]—as simple, artless, and uneducated. His writing is powerful, the prose of a man fully at home in written speech, indeed, of a master writer. He is thoroughly capable of expressing himself clearly and convincingly, and often with great beauty and originality. If he was not well read in the philosophers, nor interested in doing so, he was on the other hand steeped in the culture of the Church: the scriptures, the liturgy, the lives of the saints, and the works of the Church fathers. While direct quotations of the latter are relatively rare, and the naming of his sources even more infrequent, the reader acquainted with Greek patristic writings will recognize at once that here is an author who moves entirely in the world of their thought, and does so with an ease and confidence which speak of long familiarity.[9] Moreover, the tradition of the Greek Church is

---

7 Völker often makes this observation. See, for example, *Praxis und Theoria*, 46.

8 For example, *Vie* 20 (30).

9 It is the particular strength of Völker's work to place Symeon within the context of his predecessors and supply the reader with

so much St Symeon's bone and fiber, so at home is he within it, that in him it takes on a very special freshness and immediacy. Perhaps here his lack of the higher education available to an eleventh-century Byzantine worked both to his and the reader's advantage. There is no trace in his diction of the precious antiquarian. His language comes close at times to the spoken idiom of late Byzantium.[10] He speaks to us directly, confidently, and unspoiled by any of the longing to reproduce ancient literary models which so afflicted the prose of his learned contemporaries.

The *Ethical Discourses* represent St Symeon's single most sustained attempt to set out for a wide readership his thought on the two issues that moved him throughout both his public and private life: first, the direct experience of God in Christ as the heart of the Good News which is offered to the believer in this life and, second, its corollary, that there are those, like Symeon the Pious and our Symeon himself, who have experienced this same reality and, with it, all the charismata afforded the Apostles and great saints of the past. The Gospel is never a "deposit" for him, never something to be looked back toward. It is always contemporary, continually renewed in the Holy Spirit, and one may, rather must, live in it now just as fully as the holy ones of old. The latter enjoy no special privilege. The Apostles and saints are not "envious."[11] Their experience should be ours as well. Both they and we, modern Christians, partake of a single new reality, the Church, which is the body of Christ and presence here-below of the world to come.

It is therefore not surprising that the *Discourses* begin with an extended discussion of the Church. *Discourses* I and II comprise a unit of sorts around this theme. *Discourse* III marks a kind of transition, *via* the Eucharist, to the saint's treatises on the virtues

references to his rare citations—and far more frequent allusions.
10 See Darrouzès, *SC* 122, 76-83.
11 See Symeon on this score in *Discourse* V, volume II, forthcoming.

in *Discourses* IV through XI. The latter together make up what
Jean Darrouzès has called the New Theologian's *summa* on the
mystical life.[12] It is really nothing less than that. In these seven
treatises Symeon deals at length with the traditional virtues of the
spiritual and ascetic life. Dispassion (*apatheia*) and perfection are
covered in *Discourses* IV and VI, the conscious experience of the
Holy Spirit particularly in V, the true "service" of God (as op-
posed to merely ascetic labors) in VII, faith and the love of God
in *Discourse* VIII, the meaning of "true knowledge" as born of
grace and the Spirit in IX, what the "Day of the Lord" means in
X, and the role of "mortification," or participation in the death of
Christ, in the acquisition of the virtues in *Discourse* XI. The four
concluding discourses, XII-XV, are quite separate meditations on,
respectively, two passages from the Epistles of St Paul, on spiritual worship, and on the meaning of monastic withdrawal (*hesy-
chia*). Their tone is altogether different, without any polemical
edge or note of controversy, and they appear thus to have been
written apart from the preceding eleven, perhaps coming from a
different period in the saint's life.

Nowhere in these treatises do we find the New Theologian's
thought spelled out in a series of propositions or, save insofar as
he is the inheritor of a long prior tradition, in philosophically
refined and precise terminology. His thinking is fluid, highly
dependent on metaphor and striking image, very much a living
voice trying to come to terms with, and communicate, a lived
experience. He cannot, or better, will not confine himself in these
treatises to any one fixed literary or scholastic form. He moves
freely from theological summary to exegesis, from poetry to
polemic, from exhortation to personal witness. Yet his thinking is
not inconsistent. He makes use of a long-established vocabulary
of theological thought, of even older liturgical and ascetic tradi-

12Darrouzès, *SC* 122, 14. For all the Discourses save I-III, X and
    XIV, see volume II, forthcoming.

tions, and reads these traditional elements—which he understands very well—through the lens of his own, personal experience. But there is no conflict, let alone rupture, between the last element and the preceding ones. Symeon is not an apostle of the personal and subjective over the objective and institutional—though, as we will observe in our Introduction, he may strain certain tensions to their limits. Rather, for him Orthodoxy and the ascetic tradition serve to illumine and define his experience while the latter provides the substantiation, or proof, of the former.

Theology is nothing less than reality, to be tested and known empirically. St Symeon's writings, all of his public life, bear witness to this truth, and nowhere in all the corpus of his works does he argue for it more forcefully and at greater length than in the essays published in these volumes. The *Ethical Discourses* are indeed his *summa*, provided we take that term in the sense of a summary, a definitive statement. They are the summation of a lifelong study of the scriptures and the fathers, of an immersion in the liturgical life of the Church, and of lived experience.

On the Translation

For a novice translator, such as this writer, St Symeon presents no extraordinary difficulties, at least as compared to the lexical and syntactical complexities of a St Maximus, a Photius, or even a Gregory Palamas. As I noted just above, Symeon's prose is quite as straightforward as his thought is direct and unambiguous. Nonetheless, in adapting one language to another, any translator must make certain decisions, and the latter will necessarily always carry the possibility, not to say inevitability, of betrayal. Whether as a result of a native conservatism, or of the caution which I felt it behooved one to exercise who was embarking on a project of this scope for the first time, I have elected to keep my translation as literal a rendering of the New Theologian's Greek as I could manage without doing violence to the canons of English grammar. The result is far

from ideal. Thus, if this great writer and saint has emerged
from my hands as far more wooden and awkward in expression
than he is in his native idiom, I must take full responsibility for
it and ask both his and the reader's pardon.

Certain terms in Greek present peculiar problems for the
translator. One such, which is both notorious and frequently used,
is the word *nous* and the constellation of terms deriving from it
(*noetos, noeta, noeo*, etc.). I have followed the lead given by the
translators of the *Philokalia*[13] and have chosen to render it as
consistently as possible with the English "intellect." One could
wish there were a better choice, especially since the English word
has little or none of the sense of "Reality" clinging to it that *nous*
has in the Greek. Together with all the fathers who, from Clement
of Alexandria on, used it, Symeon means by this expression far
more than mere mentation, i.e., the faculty of rational thought and
the making of concepts. *Nous* is instead for him an equivalent for
the biblical term "heart (*kardia*)," which he also uses, and which
signifies the "center" of the human being, the highest faculty, the
very point where God and humanity are intended to meet. The
"intelligibles" (*ta noeta* or *to noeton*), as that which intellect
perceives, are thus the spiritual universe, the angels for example,
or the thoughts and intentions which God has with regard to
creation. Put another way, *nous* for Symeon is that by virtue of
which human beings may "see" the invisible. It is that in us which
enables us to respond to God's uncreated grace.

With regard to the frequent allusions to, and citations from
Scripture in the *Ethical Discourses,* I have chosen where possible
to quote the text of the RSV. This includes Symeon's frequent
references to the *Psalms*. The number of the particular psalm
quoted and verse(s) will thus be cited in the brackets according to
the RSV's numbering. In those instances, however, where the

13See the note on "intellect" in the glossary of *The Philokalia*, vol.
  I (Palmer, Sherrard, Ware), 362.

New Theologian's bible does not correspond to the Masoretic base for the RSV Old Testament, the bracketed reference will carry the Septuagint numbering together with the letters, LXX. Where Symeon is quoting loosely, paraphrasing, or conflating different texts, I have indicated this with the notation, "cf.," in the brackets preceding the text(s) alluded to. Direct citations from patristic sources are relatively rare. Where they do occur, and where I or Jean Darrouzès have been able to identify them (not possible in every instance), I have provided citations from J.P. Migne's *Patrologia Graeca* in an accompanying footnote.

Headings for the different discourses, as well as the chapter titles in *Discourses* I and II, belong to the original text and are either the work of Symeon himself, or of his editor, Nicetas Stethatos. These have been much abbreviated at my hands, for the convenience of the reader, and are printed in boldface. In smaller print, I have added an introduction to each discourse immediately above its heading and, throughout the texts, occasional subtitles in italics to lighten the reader's way.

Acknowledgements

In noting Jean Darrouzès' name just above, I am obliged to acknowledge my complete indebtedness to him for the critical text of the *Ethical Discourses* which he edited and published in the volumes 122 and 129 of *Sources chrétiennes*. His French translation, printed facing the Greek text, also provided me with occasional assistance in my own translation. It further inspired in me a lasting admiration.

Much of the research for this volume, and in particular for its introduction, I completed while enjoying a Summer Fellowship in 1991 at Dumbarton Oaks' center for Byzantine studies. The splendid library, generous office space, an atmosphere free of distractions and an ever helpful staff allowed me to accomplish more in the space of a single summer than I would have thought possible had I not experienced it. My thanks to everyone concerned there are heartfelt.

This book might well not have seen the light of print at all, or at least not for some time, had it not been for the indefatigable labors of my teaching assistant this past semester at Marquette University, Ms. Rebecca Moore. Long hours of drudgery, whether in checking references or in slaving over a word-processor, filled many of her days. For all that, and for her intelligent and useful suggestions (all accepted gladly), I am most grateful. By way of comfort and assurance, I would also like here to suggest my confidence that those books she will undoubtedly labor over in future will be all her own.

We have seen that St Symeon speaks at length and passionately about the importance of the spiritual father. I, too, can speak from experience about its importance. Thus it is to my own father in God, the Abbot Aemilianos, whose sources I discovered so often with joy and startled recognition in the New Theologian, and to his company, the brotherhood of Simonopetra on Mt. Athos where I began this translation in May of 1989, I offer this work in humble recognition of debts I can never repay. God will that everyone have such debts. They are nothing less than the taste of heaven and the beginning—God helping us and supporting our failing wills—of the world to come.

Feast of the Conception of the Mother of God
Marquette University
1992

Prologue

We are content to let the Word direct our words in whatever we say in answer to those who have ranged themselves against us, whose endlessly bitter talk would destroy anything it touched upon—even if the target were something most dear and precious. The even flow of our discourse, and the accuracy of its criticisms will thus not be our own doing, but will come from above, indeed, from the Holy Spirit Who does battle with us and Who, for all, is the One by Whom every good thing is accomplished. For the present, though, we must put aside our struggle with those others in order to see, to look over, and to examine what those things are which God has given us and, as persuaded by the divine Paul, to ask: What is the wealth [Eph 1:18] of His goodness towards us, which He gave us from the very beginning of creation? What was our creation, and how did we transgress the commandment given us and fall away from those immortal blessings? What is the present life, and what is this world under and after which everything is seen to move? And what is that which will come after for us who worship the Trinity? I will begin here, making God the beginning of my discourse.

FIRST ETHICAL DISCOURSE

Introduction

Discourse I provides the great framework for what is to follow. It is divided, presumably by Nicetas, into twelve chapters. In the first eight chapters Symeon presents a vision of sacred history spanning the sweep of time into eternity. He begins with the creation and concludes with the glory of the eschaton. Glory is, in fact, the keynote. Adam and Eve were created, he tells us in phrases recalling St Irenaeus of Lyons, to grow into the "rays" of divinity.[1] The Fall interrupted that process and required the subjugation of an innocent creation to the condition of the original sinners. Here Symeon looks particularly to Romans 8, a text he will turn to often throughout these works, and whose passage on predestination (vv. 29-30) will govern the following discourse. But God had foreseen the Fall and prepared beforehand the Incarnation of the Word for our and the whole world's salvation and renewal. Christ reverses the pattern of the Fall and completes the original, divine intention for man and the cosmos. His body is the new and renewed creation, filled with the glory of the Holy Spirit, of which the saints are members and whose splendors they anticipate in this life through, in particular, the Eucharist, together with their vision of the divine light. Symeon expands on the New Testament metaphors for the new creation. It is the Church, the New Jerusalem, the Temple of God, the Bride of Christ. The latter image and the mystical marriage, images drawn especially

1 Cf. *Adv.Haer.* IV.xx.1.3-4.7 and xxxviii-xxxix (*SC* 100, pt. 2, 490-492, and 942-973; and English, *ANF* I, 487-490, and 521-523). Compare this with *ED* I.57-66.

from Ephesians 5:23 and 27-29, are the themes of chapters nine through eleven. The saints share in the deified flesh of Christ, the same flesh which He took from the Virgin Mary at His Incarnation. The marriage theme is thus combined with the themes of mystical conception and child-bearing. Like the Theotokos, and because of her (thus her eternal primacy), the saints can be said to conceive and carry in themselves the Word made flesh.

In his concluding and longest chapter, Symeon addresses his opposition on the question of whether the saints know one another in the world to come. Here he sounds for the first time a refrain that will echo throughout the discourses (as it does all of his writings) that only those who have experienced these things are qualified to speak of them. He adds, characteristically, that his opponents obviously have not. The ecstasy of rapture, as he notes in the allegory of the prisoner (a hoary image going back to the cave in Plato's *Republic*), is characteristic of the initial experience of the new reality in Christ. As one grows into the experience of glory, however, the "territory" of the new creation becomes increasingly familiar. Thus, as surely as the saints know Christ "yonder," they know one another.

I.

ADAM AND THE CREATION OF THE WORLD

The world and Adam made before Paradise

God did not, as some people think, just give Paradise to our ancestors at the beginning, nor did He make only Paradise incorruptible. No! Instead, He did much more. Before Paradise He made the whole earth, the one which we inhabit, and everything in it. Nor that alone, but He also in five days brought the heavens and all they contain into being. On the sixth day He made Adam and established him as lord and king of all the visible creation. Neither Eve nor Paradise were yet created, but the whole world had been brought into being by God as one thing, as a kind of paradise, at once incorruptible yet material and perceptible. It was this world, as we said, which was given to Adam and to his descendants for their enjoyment. Does this seem strange to you? It should not. Pay attention to our argument, and it will show you clearly how this is so from the holy Scripture. It is written there: "In the beginning God created the heavens and the earth. The earth was without form and void" [Gen 1:1-2]. Next, the remaining creative works of God are given in exact detail, and then, after "there was evening and morning the fifth day" [v. 23], Scripture adds:

> Then God said, "Let us make man after our image, in our likeness, and let them have dominion over the fish of the sea, and over the birds of the air, and over the cattle, and over all the earth, and over every creeping thing that creeps upon the earth." So God created man after His own image...male and female He created them... [1:26-27]

Male and female, it says, not as though Eve had already come into being, but instead as she was still in Adam's side, co-existing within him. To continue:

And God blessed them, and God said to them, "Be fruitful and multiply, and fill the earth and subdue it and have dominion over the fish of the sea and the birds of the air and over every living thing that moves upon the earth." [1:28]

What might have been without the Fall

Do you see how at the very beginning God gave this whole world to man as a single paradise? For of what other earth is scripture speaking if not of this very one where we ourselves live even now, as was said before, and of none other? Thus it adds:

And God said, 'Behold, I have given you every plant yielding seed which is upon the face of all the earth, and every tree with seed in its fruit; you shall have them for food. And to every beast of the earth, and to every bird of the air, and to everything that creeps upon the earth..." [1:29-30]

Do you see how all things visible, both on the earth and in the sea, were given to Adam—and so to us who are his descendants—for enjoyment, and that not just Paradise was given to him? For in as much as He said it to Adam He was speaking to all of us, just as later He said through His living Word to His apostles, "what I say to you, I say to all" [Mk 13:37], since He knew that our race would multiply to an infinite, innumerable multitude on the earth. So, if even transgressing His commandment and being condemned to live and to die we men have grown to so great a multitude, imagine how many we might have been if there were no death: everyone who has been born from the creation of the world until now still alive, and what sort of life and way of living we might have had if we had been preserved incorruptible and immortal in an uncorrupted world, going through life without sin or sorrow, free of cares and untroubled. And imagine, too, how by progressing in God's commandments and putting into practice our good intentions we would have been led up in due time to a more perfect glory and transformation, drawing near to God and to the rays which spring from His divinity. The soul of each would have become brighter, and the physical body of each altered and changed into an immaterial and spiritual one, into something beyond the physical. How inconceivably and unspeakably great, too, would have been our joy and rejoicing in each other's company!

The Garden of Eden created later, as an image of the Eighth Day

But let me return to the matter at hand. As I said above, the whole world was given to Adam just like a single country, or like one property. God accomplished this in six days, as Scripture clearly says, for, after saying "And God made man, according to the image of God created He him, male and female created He them, and He blessed them," and what follows, it then adds these verses:

> And God saw everything that He had made, and behold, it was very good. And there was evening and there was morning, a sixth day. Thus the heavens and the earth were finished and all the host of them. And on the seventh day God finished His work which He had done, and He rested on the seventh day from all His work which He had done. [Gen 1:31-2:2]

Then, wishing to teach us how and from what God made man, Scripture summarizes the preceding theme and takes it up again: "This is the book of the generations of heaven and the earth when they were created" [Gen 2:4], and then, after a little: "And the Lord God formed man of dust from the ground," which we are to understand as meaning that He created man by taking dust from the earth "and breathed into his face the breath of life and man became a living soul" [2:7].

After showing us plainly how the world was made, God then acts like a king, or ruler, or a wealthy man. Such a person, in the country or territory which he rules, does not make all of his land a city girded by walls, nor a single fenced-in house, but instead divides it up into parts. One part he sets aside for an orchard, another for a vineyard, still another he leaves uncultivated, and in a particularly favored and beautiful spot he makes his dwelling place. Here he sets up palaces and houses, builds baths and plants gardens, and arranges for as many pleasurable things as he can imagine. Then he sets a fence around all of it, a fence with keys, and doors which open and close. Nor is the fence alone enough, but he must have guards as well lest he have any cause for fear, such that his house becomes both widely known and set apart in every way, with entry forbidden to ungrateful and scheming friends, or to quarrelsome servants (if any such undesirables should happen along), but with no hindrance given true and faithful friends, or to grateful servants, who may be permitted to come and go at will. In just this way did God act for the first man. After He had created everything out of nothing, and had made man, and had rested on the seventh day from all His works which He had made, then God planted the garden in Eden, in the East. He planted it in a particular part of the world, made a kind of royal palace, and there He placed the man whom He had made.

Why did He not make this garden He was planning on the seventh day, instead of planting it in the East only after He had made all things? Because God, Who knows everything beforehand, brought creation into being with order and harmony, and established the seven days as a type of the seven ages which would come later, and Paradise He planted afterwards as a sign of the age to come. For what reason, then, does the Holy Spirit not join this, the eighth day, to the seven preceding ones? This is because it was not fitting to reckon the eighth with the cycle of the seven. With the latter, first and second and in order all the seven circle each other in the cycle which comprises the week, in which first days are many indeed and seventh days just as numerous, but THAT day must be reckoned as wholly outside the cycle, since it has neither beginning nor end.[2] For it is not a day which at present does not exist, and which

---

2 Symeon is presenting the week of creation in Genesis 1 as an image of the history of salvation, a history which will culminate in the "eighth day" or new creation. The latter has been inaugurated by Christ and awaits its complete manifestation at the Second Coming. In this paragraph, following the lead of Gregory of Nyssa (cf. *in psalm 6*, *PG* 44.609BC), he works in a second theme by equating the seven days of the week with the cycle of time and reserving the eighth day for the image of that eternity which both preceded the present creation and which will be revealed at its conclusion: "THAT day... has neither beginning nor end." Thirdly, this preoccupation with the week of seven days and the ages of creation looks back at once to sources in ancient Greek literature—the "seven ages of man" and the four eras of human history (golden age, silver, bronze, iron; cf. Hesiod, *Works and Days*, 90-201)—and to Jewish and early Christian apocalyptic speculation which combined the notion of the different ages of history with Genesis 1 to produce the idea of the 6,000 years of creation followed by a seventh millennium of paradise restored, and then by the end of the world and the new creation (cf., for example, *I Enoch* 93, and *II Enoch* 32-33, together with D.S. Russell, *The Method and Message of Jewish Apocalyptic* [Philadelphia, 1964], esp. 286-297). While here, and especially in *Discourse* II below, Symeon does not repeat the note of precise timing typical of the popular apocalypses, he does give us seven ages which appear, roughly, to be the following: 1) Adam in Paradise, 2) the Fall to the Flood, 3) Noah to Abraham, 4) Abraham to Moses and the Law, 5) Moses to Christ, 6) Christ Himself while on earth, 7) the present era of attendance upon Christ and foretaste of the world to come obtainable in the Church, and 8) the eighth day and open manifes-

will have a beginning and come to be. Rather, it was at once before all ages, and is now, and will be for ages of ages. But it is said to have a beginning when it will come at the last and finally be revealed to us, and become within us one single day without evening and without end.

Notice that it is nowhere written, "God created paradise," or that He said "let it be, and it was," but instead that He "planted" it, and "made to grow every tree that is pleasant to the sight and good for food" [Gen 2:8-9], bearing every kind and variety of fruit, fruit which is never spoiled or lacking but always fresh and ripe, full of sweetness, and providing our ancestors with indescribable pleasure and enjoyment. For their immortal bodies had to be supplied with incorruptible food. So their way of living was untroubled and their life without weariness in the middle of that garden which the Creator had walled round about, and in which He had placed an entrance through which they could come and go.

II.

ON ADAM'S TRANSGRESSION AND EXILE

The first pair stripped of Glory and cast out of Paradise

It is thus the case that Adam was created with an incorruptible

tation of the new creation. We say "roughly" because Symeon neither accords any strictly numerical value to the different ages he sketches here (and in more detail in *Discourse* II below) nor is he entirely clear or consistent in their application. Both qualifications are scarcely surprising. The Church Fathers, with some notable exceptions (cf. especially Irenaeus of Lyons, *Adv. Haer.* V.xxviii.3, for precisely 6,000 years and following millennium), tended to avoid literal millennialism. The notion of differing "ages" was therefore, however frequently resorted to, never fixed in any definitive formula. For a thorough study of this complex subject in patristic literature, see Auguste Luneau, *L'histoire du salut chez les pères de l'Eglise: la doctrine des ages du monde* (Paris, 1964), esp. 35-206 for the Greek Fathers.

body, though one which was material and not yet spiritual, and was established by God the Creator as the immortal king of an incorrupt world, and I mean by the latter everything under heaven and not just Paradise. God had given them a law, however, commanding them not to eat of that one tree. Adam chose not to believe the words which his Maker and Lord had spoken to him: "In the day that you eat of it you shall die" [Gen 2:17], but was persuaded instead by the crooked serpent who told him: "You will not die. For God knows that when you eat of it your eyes will be opened, and you will be like God, knowing good and evil...and he ate" [3:4-6]. Immediately, he was stripped of his incorruptible vesture and glory, and clothed with the nakedness of mortality. On seeing himself naked, he hid himself and sewed together fig leaves to wrap around his waist in order to try to hide his shame. Then, when God calls to him, "Adam, where are you?" he answers, "I heard your voice and I was afraid, because I was naked; and I hid myself" [3:9-10]. And God tries to bring him to repentance by asking; "And who told you that you were naked? Have you eaten of the tree of which I commanded you not to eat?" But Adam will not admit that he has sinned. Instead, he tries to put the blame on God Who had made all things "very good," and says; "The woman whom You gave to be with me, she gave me fruit of the tree, and I ate" [3:11-12]. And the woman in her turn ascribes blame to the serpent, and because both of them absolutely would not repent and fall down before their Master to ask His forgiveness, He removes them and throws them out of the royal palace, the dwelling-place of nobility—I mean Paradise—so that they must live afterwards on this earth as foreigners and exiles.

"And immediately He ordered the flaming sword to guard the entry to the tree of life" [Gen 3:24]. This does not mean that on the future day of their restoration they are to be brought back to this perceptible and material Paradise. For the garden is not still

guarded to the present day for this reason, nor is it on this account
that God did not curse it. Rather, He wills to hold it out to us as a
type of the indissoluble life to come, an icon of the eternal
Kingdom of Heaven. If this were not the case, then the Garden,
too, would have had to be cursed, since it was the scene of the
transgression. However, God does not do this, but instead curses
all the rest of the earth which, as we have said, was incorruptible,
just like Paradise, and produced fruit of its own accord. In order
that Adam, on leaving Paradise, should not have an untroubled
life, free of labor and sweat, God cursed the earth beforehand,
saying:

> Cursed is the ground because of you; in toil you shall eat
> of it all the days of your life; thorns and thistles it shall
> bring forth to you; and you shall eat the plants of the field
> [set aside for wild beasts and dumb animals]. In the sweat
> of your face you shall eat bread till you return to the
> ground; for out of it you were taken; you are dust, and to
> dust you shall return. [3:17-19]

Whole creation subjected unwillingly to the fallen Adam

It was therefore altogether fitting that Adam, who had been
brought down to corruption and death by his own transgression,
should inhabit an earth become in like manner transitory and
mortal, and that he should worthily partake of its food. Since
unrestricted pleasure, and an incorrupt and effortless way of life
had led him to forget that every good thing had come from God,
and had brought him to despise the commandment which had
been given him, he was justly condemned to work the earth with
effort and sweat, and to draw from it, as from some niggardly
steward of an estate, his daily bread. Do you see how the earth,
now cursed and deprived of its spontaneous germination, received
the transgressor? What for and why? So that, worked by him with
labor and sweat, it should provide its fruits in a manner propor-
tionate to his needs, but, without cultivation, that it should remain

without fruit, productive only of thorns and thistles. Therefore, indeed, when it saw him leave Paradise, all of the created world which God had brought out of non-being into existence no longer wished to be subject to the transgressor. The sun did not want to shine by day, nor the moon by night, nor the stars to be seen by him. The springs of water did not want to well up for him, nor the rivers to flow. The very air itself thought about contracting itself and not providing breath for the rebel. The wild beasts and all the animals of the earth saw him stripped of his former glory and, despising him, immediately turned savagely against him. The sky was moving as if to fall justly down on him, and the very earth would not endure bearing him upon its back.

What then? God Who created all and made man, Who knew before the world was made that Adam would transgress the commandment, and Who had fore-ordained the man's re-birth and re-creation through the birth into the flesh of His only-begotten Son, what does God do here? He Who holds all things together by His own power and compassion and goodness, now suspends the assault of all creation, and straightway subjects all of it to Adam as before. He wills that creation serve man for whom it was made, and like him become corruptible, so that when again man is renewed and becomes spiritual, incorruptible, and immortal, then creation, too, now subjected to the rebel by God's command and made his slave, will be freed from its slavery and, together with man, be made new, and become incorruptible and wholly spiritual. For this is what the all-compassionate God and Lord had fore-ordained from before the foundation of the world.

Adam's descendants defile creation with idolatry

After these things had come to pass thus because of God's wisdom, Adam, cast out of Paradise, begot his children, lived his life, and died. So likewise did his descendants do. The men of that time had a recent memory of the Fall, being taught about it in any case by Adam and Eve, and they therefore held God in reverence and honored Him as their Master. It was on account of this reverence that Abel and Cain offered sacrifices of their possessions to God. It is written that God accepted the offering and sacrifice of Abel, but not yet that of Cain. And Cain, knowing this, was grieved unto death, it is said, and from there was led even to the envy and murder of his brother. Enoch, however, later so pleases God that he is taken away by Him from the earth, as Elijah is carried up afterwards in the fiery chariot. In these latter instances God showed that if, even after His decision against Adam and Adam's seed was carried out, if, even after Adam's exile, the latter's sons should prove well-pleasing to Him, then He would honor them with a translation from the earth or with long life. Now, if He delivered them from corruption, that is, from returning to the earth and descending into hell—them who were afterwards fated to die or, more truly speaking, be transformed—then how much greater would Adam's glory and honor and welcome with God have been if he had not transgressed the commandment, or, if transgressing, had repented and been allowed to remain in Paradise?

Thus for years knowledge about God was transmitted through a succession of teachers, and the ancients recognized their Creator. Later, though, when men had multiplied, and from their youth had turned their thoughts to evil, they were dragged down to forgetfulness and ignorance of the God Who had made them, and worshipped not only idols and demons as gods, but even deified that very creation which God had given them for their service. They gave themselves up to every debauchery and unclean activity, soiling the earth, the air, the sky, and everything beneath it by their unnatural practices. For nothing else so soils the work of God and makes unclean what is clean as the deification of creation and the worshipping of it as equal to God the Creator and Maker. Thus all creation, defiled now and worshipped by man, is soiled and brought down to complete corruption. When, therefore, wickedness was complete, and all were imprisoned together in disobedience, according to the holy Apostle [Rom 11:32], then God, the Son of God, descended upon earth to re-fashion the one who had been broken, to bring him to life who had died, and to call His own creature back from delusion.

Now, pay attention, I beg you, to my exact words here, for I would have this treatise be useful to future generations. We will require the use of images in order to contemplate the Incarnation of the Word and His ineffable birth from Mary the ever-Virgin, and in order to know truly the mystery of the economy from on high, which was hidden before the ages, for the salvation of the world.

III.

ON THE INCARNATION OF THE WORD

Christ from Mary as Eve from Adam

It was in the way that God of old fashioned our mother, Eve, when He took the rib from Adam's already living side and built it up into the woman—for it was on account of this that He did not breathe on it, as with Adam, the breath of life; rather, with the part which He took from his flesh, He completed the whole body of the woman, and the first fruits of the Spirit already present in the living flesh He made into a living soul, having indeed already created both as man at the same time—in just the same fashion, taking living flesh from the holy Theotokos and ever-Virgin Mary as a kind of leaven and first-fruit from the dough of our common nature—soul and body both—God the Maker and Fashioner united it with His own incomprehensible and unapproachable divinity. Rather, it was with our essence that He united essentially the whole substance [*hypostasis*] of His divinity, mingling unmingeldly the one with the Other, the human with His own, building it up into a temple consecrated to Himself. Thus, without alteration or change, did the Creator of Adam become Himself perfect man.

Just as He made the woman from the man's side, as we said above, just so He borrows flesh from Adam's daughter, Mary the Theotokos and ever-Virgin, and, having adopted it, is born without seed like the first man. So that, as Adam was through his transgression the source of birth into corruption and death, just so may Christ God become through the fulfilling of all righteousness the first-fruits of our re-fashioning in incorruption and of our immortality. This is what the divine Paul means when he says:

> The first man was from the earth, a man of dust; the second
> man is from heaven. As was the man of dust, so are those
> who are of the dust; and as is the man of heaven, so are
> those who are of heaven. [I Cor 15:47-48]

And elsewhere he writes: "Christ is the first-fruits, then are those who are Christ's" [I Cor 15:23]. Thus, because He took, in both body and soul, the title of perfect man, became like us in every respect except for sin, through our faith in Him He imparts to us from His own divinity. He even makes us kin to the nature and essence of His divinity. Look with me at the novelty and paradox of this mystery! God the Word, Who by nature has no flesh, took from us and became man, which He was not before. He imparts His own divinity to those who believe in Him—something which neither angels nor men had ever had before—and, by adoption and by grace, they become gods who before were not. It is thus that He gives them "power to become sons of God" [Jn 1:12], and that is why they become such, and are ever becoming such, and shall know no end to their becoming such. Listen to St Paul saying the same: "Just as we have borne the image of the man of dust, we shall also bear the image of the man of heaven" [I Cor 15:49]. Enough on this subject, let us take up again the thread of our discourse.

The sequence of salvation: first the soul is redeemed, then the body

Since, through His coming in the body, God came to earth to

re-fashion man and to renew him, and in addition to bless all of creation which on account of man had been accursed—listen well!—He first vivified the soul which He had taken and, making it incorruptible, deified it. His immaculate and divine body, though also deified, He yet wore still as a corruptible and material thing. For eating and drinking, toil and sweat, being chained and beaten, and finally being hung up nailed to the cross are obviously corruptible and material. All these things comprise properties of a mortal body, on which account He both died and was laid dead in the tomb. But, when He had risen incorruptible from the dead, He also raised up His body as wholly divine, spiritual and immaterial. We know this from the fact that He did not break the seals of the tomb on leaving it, and that He both entered and departed the upper room without hindrance through doors which were closed. And why did He not render the body right away spiritual and incorruptible with the soul when He assumed them both? This is because Adam, when he ate from the tree which God had forbidden him to eat of, suffered the death of his soul as soon as he transgressed, but that of the body only many years later. Christ therefore first raised up, vivified, and deified the soul which had suffered first the punishment of death, and then, to the body condemned by the ancient judgment to return to the earth in death, He granted the reception of incorruptibility through the Resurrection. Nor is this all, but descending into hell He freed the souls of the saints held captive there in everlasting bonds, and raised them up, and established them in a place of refreshment and of light without evening—not yet, indeed, their bodies, for those He suffered to remain in the grave until the general resurrection.

This mystery, however, did not just occur in the manner described once for all time in Christ, but it has also occurred in the case of each one of the saints of old, and it still continues to happen always, even to the present day. This is so because, when we receive the Spirit of our Master and God, we become participants of His divinity and essence, and when we eat of His all-pure

flesh—I mean the holy communion—we become truly His kin, of
one body with Him. It is just as St Paul himself says, that "we are
bone of His bones and flesh of His flesh" [cf. Eph 5:30], and again
that "of the fullness of His divinity have we"—that is, all of
us—"received, and grace upon grace" [Jn 1:16 and Col 2:9].
When this occurs, we become by grace like our Master, God, the
Lover of humanity. We are renewed, our soul is made new. We
are made incorruptible, as if we had already been raised, living,
from the dead. This is to say, we see Him Who deigned to become
like us, and we are seen by Him who have been made worthy of
becoming like Him. It is as if someone were to see the face of a
friend from far off, and speak to him, and converse with him, and
hear his voice.

It is therefore thus that the saints for ages, both those of old
and those who now have spiritual sight, see no shape or form or
impression, but formless light, in as much as they themselves have
taken on the quality of light, in the light of the Holy Spirit. When
each of the saints arrives at this condition, it is not as if his body
becomes immediately incorruptible and spiritual. Rather, like iron
burning in the fire partakes of the latter's brilliance and loses its
dark coloring, then, when taken away from the forge, turns cold
and dark again, so in fact do the bodies of the saints partake of the
divine fire, and are sanctified, and burn incandescent, and become
themselves translucent, and are restored as more excellent, more
precious by far, than other bodies. When, though, the soul departs
and is separated from the body of the saint, [his body] is immediately given over to corruption and begins shortly to dissolve. But
still, such bodies may remain for many years, neither wholly
incorrupt nor again quite corrupted, but keeping yet the indica-
tions each of corruption and incorruption, being preserved for the
final resurrection when they shall be made perfectly new and
incorruptible.

Our bodies await the restoration of the whole creation

Why is this? It is so because it was not fitting that men's bodies should be restored and made incorruptible before the renewal of all the creation. Instead, just as the created world was first brought into existence as incorrupt, and then later, man, so again it is creation which must first be transformed from corruption into incorruption, changed, and then, together with it and at the same time, the corrupted bodies of men will be renewed, such that, himself become at once spiritual and immortal, man may have an incorrupt, and spiritual, and everlasting country in which to make his home. Listen to the Apostle Peter for the truth of this:

> The day of the Lord will come like a thief in the night, and then the heavens shall burn and be dissolved, and the elements melt away with fire [II Pet 3:10].

This does not mean that they shall be destroyed, but rather re-forged and transmuted into a greater and everlasting condition. Where do we know this from? From, again, the words of the same Apostle, where he says: "According to his promise, we wait for new heavens and a new earth" [II Pet 3:13]. Whose promise is this? Certainly it is the promise of Christ our God. He said: "Heaven and earth shall pass away, but my words shall not pass away" [Mt 24:35]. By "passing away" He means "change," for even if heaven should be changed, He says, My words will remain fixed and unchanging. Long ago David the prophet proclaimed the same when he said: "And You shall roll them up like a curtain, and they shall be changed; but You are the same, and Your years shall not fail" [Ps 102:26-27]. What could be more clear than these words?

But, now it is time for us to examine how creation shall be renewed and restored to its original beauty.

IV.

CREATION MADE NEW

When the Apostle promises therefore a new heaven and a new earth, none of the faithful will contradict him, nor will anyone doubt that the Lord said the same as well. Just as our bodies, although they dissolve for a time, do not pass away forever, but will be renewed again at the resurrection, so, too, will heaven and earth and all that is within them—that is, all of creation—be made anew and liberated from the bondage of corruption. The elements themselves will share with us in that incandescence from above, and in the same way that we shall be tried by fire, so, according to the Apostle, shall all creation be renewed through fire. We may learn this from the Apostle Peter, who writes:

> But the day of the Lord will come like a thief in the night, and then the heavens will pass away with a loud noise, and the elements will be dissolved with fire, and the earth and the works that are upon it will be burned up. [II Pet 3:10]

Do you see how he says that everything will be re-forged and changed by fire? Therefore he adds: "Since all these things are thus to be dissolved, what sort of persons ought you to be in lives of holiness and godliness" [3:11]. How, then, are all things to be dissolved? In just the way that a copper vessel, when it has grown old and become quite spoiled and useless on account of rust, is taken by the craftsman and put in the fire to be re-forged by him and formed again as new. In the same way, creation, too, after having grown old and been spoiled by our sins, is dissolved in fire by the Maker of all, and then forged anew and transmuted, and becomes incomparably brighter and newer than the world which we see now.

After writing of these things, the Apostle Peter says a little later:

> Therefore, beloved, since you wait for these, be zealous to
> be found by Him without spot or blemish, and at peace.
> And count the forbearance of our Lord as salvation. So
> also our beloved brother Paul wrote to you according to
> the wisdom given him, speaking of this as he does in all his
> letters. There are some things in them hard to understand,
> which the ignorant and unstable twist to their own destruc-
> tion, as they do the other scriptures. [II Pet 3:14-16]

Now, this does not just apply to people then, but to the majority
today. Indeed, just about all of us suffer from speaking out of
ignorance. We mix everything up. We twist the whole of holy
Scripture to our own damnation by misinterpreting it. It is as if
we try to make Scripture an accomplice in our own passions,
our lusts, and our perdition.

Let us look instead at what St Paul says about creation and its
renewal. He writes that "I consider that the sufferings of the present
time are not worth comparing with the glory that is to be revealed to
us," and adds: "For the creation waits with eager longing for the
revealing of the sons of God" [Rom 8:18-19]. By "eager longing" he
means burning desire, and by "revealing" he means its manifestation
in the resurrection. At that time, by virtue of the second coming of
Christ our God, the sons of God must be revealed and their beauty
appear fully as what in truth they are. So it is written: "Then the
righteous will shine like the sun" [Mt 13:43]. It is clear that these are
the sons of the righteous God. And in order that you not fancy that
the Apostle is talking about some other creation, he adds a little later:
"For the creation was subjected to futility, not of its own will but by
the will of Him Who subjected it in hope" [Rom 8:20].

Do you see how it is not without reason that I said earlier that
creation no longer wished to serve the transgressor, Adam, since
it saw him as one who had fallen from divine glory and rebelled
against his own Maker? This is the reason why, when God saw
from before the creation of the world that Adam would be saved
through re-birth, He subjected creation to him, and put it under a

curse so that, having been created for the sake of man who had
fallen into corruption, it should itself become corrupt and provide
him annually with corrupted food. But then, when God makes
man new again and renders him immortal, incorruptible and
spiritual, at that time, I say, He will change all of creation itself
together with man, and will bring it to completion as immaterial
and everlasting. For this is what the Apostle meant when he said,
"The creation was subject to futility, not of its own will, but by the
will of Him Who subjected it in hope." Which is to say that
creation was not of itself subjected to humanity, nor was it willingly changed over to corruption and made to bear perishable
fruits and to sprout thorns and thistles, but as obedient to God's
command Who ordered these things, and with the hope of a
restoration. Wishing to make this still more clear, St Paul adds:
"Because the creation will be set free from its bondage to decay
and obtain the glorious liberty of the children of God"
[Rom 8:21].

V.

THE ULTIMATE SPLENDOR OF CREATION

It will be changed

However renewed, creation will not return to what it was
created in the beginning. God forbid! Rather, just as it is sown
a "natural body," according to the saying [I Cor 15:44], so it is
raised a body, not like the first man's before the transgression—i.e., material, perceptible, and mutable, requiring moreover physical food—but instead a body wholly spiritual and
immutable; such a body as that of our Master and God after His
resurrection, the body of the Second Adam, Who is our first
born from the dead [Col 1:18]. As His body was a far different
thing than the old Adam's, so shall the whole creation, in the
same way and at God's command, not become what it was

before, material and perceptible, but be transformed in the re-birth into an immaterial, spiritual dwelling place, beyond any perception of the senses. As St Paul says in a different way: "We shall not all sleep, but we shall all be changed, in a moment, in the twinkling of an eye" [I Cor 15:51-52]. So shall creation be set aflame by the divine fire and changed, that the word of the prophet may be fulfilled which says: "The righteous shall inherit the land" [Ps 37:29]. This certainly does not mean the perceptible earth, for how could that be, seeing that they lay claim to becoming spiritual, but an altogether spiritual and immaterial world, one where the righteous may be, as it were, embodied in a bodiless way, may enter into a perception which transcends the senses, and, themselves circumscribed, may be as uncircumscribed among the uncircumscribed beings, and so possess a dwelling place worthy of their glory.

Angels and souls are created spirits

Now, then, try to imagine with me a world which is spiritual and rises beyond our perception. But, what is beyond sensible perception and spiritual is quite incomprehensible for us, and invisible. So, how could we define what is neither seen nor grasped in any way, or who in his right mind would try? No one, of course! It is in this sense, therefore, that we can discourse about the angels, i.e., that they are also, in effect, somehow embodied and circumscribable, at least when compared to the absolutely immaterial and bodiless nature of divinity. St Paul thus writes: "There are celestial bodies and there are terrestrial bodies" [I Cor 15:40], these here on earth being material, and those above us immaterial. Elsewhere the Scripture says: "He Who makes His angels spirits and His ministers a flame of fire" [Ps 104:4]. Since, then, the heavenly minds are spirits who perform a ministry, are sent out to do service, as appears to be the case according to St Paul, our initiator into these matters, then it follows that when a holy angel is sent down from above, from God, by the latter's command, he leaves behind the heavenly choirs and enters into relation with the earthly and with us, as all agree. If this statement be in conformity with truth as generally understood, then the angel appears in this instance to be circumscribed and definable. In comparison with the divine and uncreated nature which is bodiless and uncircumscribed in every respect, the angel is revealed as created and circumscribed. Relative to our nature, however, they are wholly bodiless, ungraspable, and invisible.

The same reasoning holds for the soul as well. Compared to God Who is by nature bodiless, and to the angels, the soul is as it were somehow bodily and circumscribed, but it is such only with respect to Him Who is able to bind it and Who has the authority to cast it together with the body into the hell of fire. For mortal perception, however, it is altogether bodiless and incomprehensible, nor is it possible to circumscribe it within any physical place or space whatsoever. Let no one be astonished at hearing this. Let him rather reflect on how the bodiless angels come and go invisibly through closed doors, and how the same receive the souls of men [at death]. Let him listen to the Lord saying: "In the resurrection they neither marry nor are given in marriage, but are like the angels in heaven" [Mt 22:30]; and to St Paul, who writes: "It is sown a physical body, it is raised a spiritual body" [I Cor 15:44]; and let him learn from these sources precisely that our bodies are going to become spiritual, so to speak like the angels, when we are raised from the dead. For if they are sown physical and raised spiritual, as the Scripture has it, and if we are to be like God's angels in the coming age, as our Lord Himself says, then it is clear that we shall be similar to them, if not in nature then in dignity. As I said, relative to God the angels are embodied, just as compared to us they are immaterial and invisible. But if this is so, then the rule and application of this comparison applies all the more to souls.

Heaven and earth will be joined in Christ

Having entered into such a state of being at the resurrection, as our argument has demonstrated, and having thus become spiritual and graduated to a level beyond all perception of the senses as being like God's angels, if not in nature then in dignity, what remaining need shall we have of any perceptible earth and dwelling place? Now, it is the dignity of the angels, and both their state of being and their desire, to be as secondary lights reflecting the primary and divine light, to look on the glory and splendor of the unapproachable and infinite light itself, and to enjoy the inexpressible Godhead in Three Persons. As I have said several times, all creation, too, once made new, will become spiritual, and together with paradise will be transformed into an immaterial, unchanging, eternal, and intelligible dwelling place. The sky on the one hand will be incomparably brighter, in a manner indeed quite new, other and brighter than our visible sky, while the earth on the other hand will take on a new and inexpressible beauty, an unfading verdure, ornamented by shining flowers, varied and spiritual. It will be an earth in which, as the sacred word has it, righteousness will have its dwelling place [II Pet 3:13]. The sun of righteousness will shine sevenfold more brightly, and the moon will gleam twice as bright as the sun which illumines it now. The stars will be like our sun—if, indeed, these are the same stars as are spoken of in the sublime thoughts of the wise. All things there are beyond speech, transcend thought, save only that they are spiritual and divine, joined to the intelligible world, and comprise another, intellectual paradise and heavenly Jerusalem, made like and united to the angelic world, the inviolable inheritance of the sons of God. Of this city no one on earth has ever been the rightful heir, nor dwelt there, nor ever set foot there. For we have all become sojourners, and so we remain, and so shall we always be on this earth, as the whole Scripture makes clear to us.

When therefore all things earthly shall be united with the

heavenly, then shall the righteous inherit this earth made new, the earth which the meek, whom our Lord declared blessed, have as their inheritance. For now, some things are united with the heavenly while others await their turn. On one hand, as we said above, the souls of the saints adhere to God while still in the body, by grace of the Holy Spirit and of their union with Him. Then, after falling asleep, their souls are renewed, and changed, and raised from death, and established again in great glory in the light without evening. Their bodies, on the other hand, are not yet glorified, but are left for the time being in the tombs and in corruption. They, too, shall be made incorruptible in the general resurrection when, of a surety, the whole earthly creation, this visible and perceptible world, will be changed and united with the heavenly, i.e., with the invisible world which transcends sensation.

This must all be accomplished first of all, and then shall come with great glory and power our longed-for and sweetest King, Jesus, Who is God and Christ, Who will judge the world and render to each according to his works. And then, as in a great mansion or royal palace where there are many rooms where one may rest and sojourn, and where there are great differences among the rooms although all are splendid, so in this new creation will our Lord make distinctions, apportioning to each his inheritance according to his worthiness, and according to the radiance and splendor which is proper to each from his virtues and his works. Given that these things are spiritual, translucent, and joined to the divine abiding and rest, it follows that the Kingdom of Heaven is entirely like—rather, is in fact—a single great hearth, as shall be clear to all the righteous. It possesses the King of all, everywhere and uniquely visible to all, dwelling with each one, and uniting each to Himself, and shining in each, and making each to shine in Himself. But woe, then, to those who are found outside that mansion!

Now that we have spoken enough, and sufficiently, about these matters, and having informed those who are not tempted to contradict us just for the sake of a quarrel, allow us to turn and provide you with solid teaching—so far as is possible—concerning how all the saints are united to Christ and become one with Him.

VI.

HOW THE SAINTS ARE UNITED TO CHRIST

As members of His body

If it is true that the saints become genuinely the members of Christ Who is God of all, and if, as we said, they have as their duty remaining attached and united to His body so that He may be their Head and they—all the saints from the beginning of the world until the Last Day—may be His members, and the many become one body of Christ, as it were a single Man, then it follows that some, for example, fulfill the role of His hands, working even now to accomplish His all-holy will, making worthy the unworthy and preserving them for Him. Others are the shoulders, bearing the burdens of others, or even carrying the lost sheep whom they find wandering in the crags and wild places abandoned by God. These, too, accomplish His will. Others fulfill the role of the breast, pouring out God's righteousness to those who hunger and thirst for it, providing them with the bread which nourishes the powers of heaven. Others still are the belly. They embrace everyone with love. They carry the Spirit of salvation in their bowels and possess the capacity to bear His ineffable and hidden mysteries. Others, again, take the function of the thighs since they carry in themselves the fecundity of the concepts adequate to God of the mystical theology. They engender the Spirit of Wisdom upon the earth, i.e., the fruit of the Spirit and His seed in the hearts of men, through the word of their teaching. Finally, there are those who act as the legs and feet. These last reveal courage

and endurance in temptations, after the manner of Job, and
their stability in the good is in no way shaken or weakened, but
instead they bear up under the burden of the Spirit's gifts.[3]

As the Church: place of the Glory

Thus is the body of Christ's Church bound together in harmony by His saints from the beginning of the world. It is complete
and entire in the union of the sons of God, the first-born, whose
names are inscribed in heaven. It is to them that God says even
now: "Do not rejoice in this, that the demons are subject to
you"—which in the frivolous creates rather vanity and presump-
tion—"but rejoice that your names are written in heaven" [Lk
10:20]. I shall endeavor to prove from the Holy Scriptures that all
the saints are members of Christ, are in process of becoming one
body with Him, and that this process will continue indefinitely.
Listen first of all to our Savior and God Himself, to how He
reveals the union with Himself to be unbreakable and indivisible
when He says to His Apostles: "I am in my Father, and you in Me,
and I in you" [Jn 14:20], and again: "I do not pray for these only,
but also for all who believe in Me through their word, that they
may all be one" [Jn 17:20-21]. Wishing to assure them concerning
the mode of union, He takes up the theme again: "Even as You,
Father, are in Me, and I in You, that these also may be one in Us"
[Jn 17:21]. Making it still more clear, He adds:

> The glory which You have given Me I have given to them,
> that they may be one even as We are one, I in them and
> You in Me, that they may be perfectly one. [Jn 17:22-23]

3 This extended image building on St Paul's description of the
  Church as the "body of Christ" (e.g. Rom 12:4-5), is paralleled
  in *Discourse IV* by Symeon's equation of the different virtues
  with the limbs and organs of the human body in his picture of
  "the complete man in Christ." The parallelism is not accidental.
  The Church and the individual Christian reflect each other as
  macrocosm and microcosm, the great world and the small.

And a little later:

> Father, I desire that they also, whom You have given Me,
> may be with Me where I am, that they may behold My
> glory, which You have given Me [Jn 17:24]

And again: "That the love with which You have loved Me may
be in them, and I in them" [Jn 17:26]. Do you see the depths of
this mystery? Do you understand the infinite transcendence of
super-abounding glory? Do you grasp that the mode of this
union transcends our intelligence and our every concept?

O, brothers, the wonder! O, the inexpressible condescension
of that love for us of God Who loves mankind! The union which
He has by nature with the Father He promises that we may have
with Him by grace, if we desire it, and that we may be in the same
relation with respect to Him, if we keep His commandments. O,
fearful promise! that the glory which the Father gave the Son, the
Son gives in turn even to us by divine grace. And yet more: that
as He is in the Father, and the Father in Him, so, if we so will, the
Son of God will be in us and we in Him by grace. O, grace
unsurpassed! that the love with which God the Father loved His
only-begotten Son and our God, that the same love will be, He
says, in us, and that He Himself, the Son of God, will be in us. And
this follows naturally, for now He has become our kinsman in the
flesh, and has rendered us co-participants in His divinity, and so
has made us all His kinsmen. Above all, the divinity imparted to
us through this communion cannot be broken down into parts, is
indivisible, and thus all of us who partake of it in truth must
necessarily and inseparably be one body with Christ in the one
Spirit.

One Glory in one Christ and one Spirit

For confirmation that this is all true, listen to St Paul: "For in
Christ Jesus there is neither slave nor free, nor Jew nor Greek, nor
Scythian, nor barbarian, but Christ is all in all" [Col 3:11]. Notice
how he does not say that "all are Christians," in the plural, but says

instead "Christ" is one, as from many members the body is one.
Listen to him again, clarifying this point elsewhere, for he says
first: "To each is given the manifestation of the Spirit for the
common good" [I Cor 12:7]; then he enumerates the charisms of
the Spirit, then adds: "But all these are effected by one and the
same Spirit Who apportions to each one individually as He wills"
[I Cor 12:11]. After he has acquainted us with the energies of the
Spirit which are given to the saints who are the members of Christ,
he adds:

> For just as the body is one and has many members, and all
> the members of the body, though many, are one body, so it
> is with Christ. For by one Spirit were we all baptized into
> one body—Jews or Greeks, slaves or free—and all were
> made to drink the one drink. For the body does not consist
> of one member but of many. [I Cor 12:12-14]

Once again, as we said above, in the same way that God gives
to each his inheritance in the pure mansions of heaven according to each one's worthiness, so in the body of the Church shall
each be reckoned as in the portion of Christ as he is worthy of
it. A little later in the same epistle, the Apostle makes this clear
when he says: "But God has arranged the members in the body,
each one of them, as He chose...for while there are many parts,
yet one body" [I Cor 12:18, 20]. In order to show the differences among the members, who and what they are, he says:

> Now you are the body of Christ and individually members
> of it. And God has appointed in the church first apostles,
> second prophets, third teachers, then powers, then graces
> of healing, of assistance, of administration, and of differ-
> ent languages. [I Cor 12:27-28]

Did you note the differences among the members of Christ?
Did you learn who His members are? Now listen as well to how
this apostle, following the Master, makes clear the unity of the
members.

The bride of Christ

Our Lord taught that we may be united to Him somewhat in the way that He is united to His Father. His disciple and apostle describes the union in terms of that which a man has with his wife, and the woman with the man. He says thus:

> Wives, be subject to your husbands, as to the Lord. For the husband is the head of the wife as Christ is head of the Church, His body, and is Himself its Savior. [Eph 5:23]

And again:

> Husbands, love your own wives, just as Christ loved the Church, and gave Himself up for her, that He might sanctify her...and present the Church to himself in splendor, without spot or wrinkle or any such thing, that she might be holy and undefiled. [Eph 5:25-27]

And yet more a little later—and pay attention, I beg you, to the depths of this saying:

> He who loves his own wife loves himself. For no man ever hates his own flesh, but nourishes it and cherishes it, as Christ does the Church, because we are members of His body, of His flesh and of His bones. [Eph 5:28-30]

See how he shows us that, just as Eve was taken from the flesh and bones of Adam and the two were one flesh, so also Christ gives Himself to us to the extent of communion of His flesh and bones. He showed them to His apostles, saying: "Handle Me and see, for a spirit has not flesh and bones as you see that I have" [Lk 24:39]. From the same flesh and bones He gives us to eat, and through this communion makes us, too, one with Him. Again the Apostle, wanting to make God's contact with us absolutely clear, adds: "For this reason a man shall leave his father and mother," meaning that he leaves them for the sake of Christ, "and is joined to his wife", that is, the Church, "and the two shall become one flesh" [Eph 5:31], clearly, he means the flesh of Christ God.

And to show that the text is to be interpreted in this sense, and
that we do not arrive at this meaning through forced reasoning, the
Apostle adds: "This mystery is a profound one, and I am saying
that it refers to Christ and the Church" [Eph 5:32]. Truly, therefore, this mystery is great—and beyond great!—and so it will
always be, because the same sort of communion, and union, and
intimacy, and kinship, which the woman has with the man and the
man with the woman, such—understood in a manner adequate to
God and as transcending our reason—is the relation which the
Master and Maker of all has with all the Church, as with a single
woman: blamelessly, ineffably, inseparably, and indivisibly
united to her, being and living with her as with the one whom He
loves and holds dear. Thus in turn the Church, united to her most
dear God, joins herself to Him as the whole body to its own head.
As a body cannot live at all without being attached to its head, then
neither can the Church of the faithful—I say, rather, of the sons of
God whose names are inscribed in heaven—in any way be a
proper and whole body for God without her head, Christ God
Himself, nor can she live the true and imperishable life without
being fed by Him with her daily and substantial bread. From the
latter comes life and growth into the perfect man, into the full
measure of the stature of His fullness [Eph 4:13], for all those who
love Him.

Now that we have clearly demonstrated these matters, and our
discourse has clearly resolved the question posed, that the saints
who have been from the beginning of the world until now, and
from now until the end of the world, must together comprise a
single body with and in Christ, let us move right along to discuss
how the world above must be filled. But, open up the ears of your
mind and be ready to pay close attention to what we have to say,
especially since at every point of our discourse we are treating of
things which are divine.

VII.

HOW THE WORLD ABOVE MUST BE FILLED

The New Creation is the Church

We must ask first of all what this world is which must be filled, and without whose filling the end will not come, and then ask what precisely we mean by "the end." It seems to me that the fully ripened world is the Church of Christ, indeed, the whole man himself, in whom God is said to dwell and to walk [II Cor 6:16], and upon whom God, the sun of righteousness, sends down the bright rays of His charisms. It is she whom we know to call the body of Christ and His bride. So Paul, conducting her to the Bridegroom, cries: "I betrothed you to Christ to present you as a pure virgin to her one Husband" [II Cor 11:2], and the divine David, too: "The queen stood at Your right hand, in clothing worked with gold, in many colored robes" [Ps 45:13-14]. While this passage is, indeed, said to refer only to the Theotokos, still it also has very properly to do with the Church of her Son and God. The following words of David make this very clear. He says:

> Virgin souls shall be brought up behind her and led to the King. The souls accompanying her shall be led in gladness and in joy; they shall be led to the temple of the King. [Ps 45:14-15]

So what do you think this temple is? Do you think that the dwelling and the temple are anything other than the King Himself? Of course not! Just as Christ is head of the Church, and God, so He becomes Himself her temple, too [cf. Rev 21:21], and in turn the Church is established as herself His temple and His fully ripened world. What I have said above makes this very clear, but let me take it up again in order to make the explanation still more exact.

What am I talking about? The words which Christ God Him-

self said to His own Father concerning both all believers and about
His own disciples: "I do not pray for these only, but also for those
who believe in Me through their word, that they may all be one" [Jn
17:20-21]. How "one"? "As You, Father, are in Me, and I in You,
that they may also be one in Us" [Jn 17:21]. Do you see how He
establishes Himself as both King and Temple of all those who are
saved? Therefore, learn again how all the faithful, the queen and
those who follow in her train, shall become the temple and world of
our God and King. And learn it first from Christ the King Himself.
For He says: "I in them and You, Father, in Me; that they may be
made perfect in one" [Jn 17:23]. And what does His disciple, Paul,
say? "Do you not know that you are God's temple and that God's
Holy Spirit dwells in you?" [I Cor 3:16]. Do you see how the
Apostle's words sing in exact harmony with those of the Master?
They demonstrate that the temple of God the King, His city and
world, is the Church. Know that it is He Who spoke in the prophets
and Apostles, and that it is He Who speaks in both of them even now!

VIII.

THE FORE-ORDAINED[4]

The Church is the body of Christ, His bride, the world to
come, and the temple of God. The members of His body are all
the saints. However, not all of the saints who will please God have
yet appeared, nor yet is the whole body of Christ thus complete,
nor the world to come yet filled. I say this about God's Church.
There are, though, many unbelievers in the world today who will
believe in Christ; many sinners and debauched who will repent
and change their lives; many undecided who will be per-
suaded.There are many, a great many, up to the sound of the last
trumpet, who will prove well-pleasing to God and who have not
yet been born. All those who are foreknown by God must be born,

4 The problem of "fore-ordination," or predestination, is taken up in
  Discourse II below, parts 1-2 and 7, pp. 83-95 and 113-115.

come into being, before the world beyond our world, the world of the Church, of the first-born, of the heavenly Jerusalem, is filled up. Then shall the end come and the fulness of the body of Christ be complete, through those who are fore-ordained by God to become conformed to the image of His Son. They are the sons of light and of His day.

These are then the fore-ordained who are inscribed and numbered, who shall be added and joined to the body of Christ. And then, when as it were the whole is realized, when no member is lacking, then shall it be fulfilled, completed, as in truth it appeared to the Apostle Paul when he said:

> Until we all attain to...a perfect man, to the measure of the stature of the fulness of Christ...[Eph 4:13] ...Those whom He foreknew those He also fore-ordained. Whom He fore-ordained, these also He called. Whom He called, He made righteous. Whom He made righteous, these also He glorified, making them conform to the image of His Son. [Rom 8:29-30]

Do you see how all the saints are both known beforehand and fore-ordained? Next, then, learn how they are all inscribed. For he says:

> You have come to Mount Zion, to the city of the living God, the heavenly Jerusalem, and to innumerable angels in festal gathering, and to the assembly of the first-born whose names are enrolled in heaven. [Heb 12:23]

If therefore they are enrolled, it follows that they are numbered. As it is written, "The Lord knows His own" [II Tim 2:19]. And there is another venerable saying: "Even the hairs of your head," He says, "are numbered" [Mt 10:30]. If even the hairs of our head are numbered by God Who knows all things, then how much more are not we? So all the saints are known long beforehand by God, are at once fore-ordained and numbered, as well as enrolled by name in heaven, and are both members of Christ and called to become and complete one body with Him. It is therefore manifest that once they are all gathered into the single body which is Christ, then the higher world, the heavenly Jerusalem itself which is the Church of the first-born, will be complete. The whole body of the queen, the Church of God and of Christ God, will be realized.

So where are those who, to their own perdition, vainly imagine many mansions outside the Kingdom of Heaven? Where are those who say: "We do not want to enter the Kingdom of Heaven, because it is too much to ask, but would rather be sufficed with a place of rest"? All the saints from the beginning must be one body with Christ! Where else do such people think they will go if they are found to be unworthy of His body and cut off from it? When the whole world is renewed by fire, where do they imagine they could ever hide so as to avoid being touched by that fire, and tested by it? Truly: "They have become futile in their thinking, and their senseless hearts have been darkened. Claiming to be wise, they have become fools" [Rom 1:12-22].

But let us proceed to the examination of the mystical marriage of God. From there we can direct our inquiry to another question. Which is that? Something which certain of the uninitiates say they want to learn, to wit: "In the age to come, when God renders to each according to his works, will the saints know one another or not?" We must begin first with the sayings of the Gospels, and from there our discourse will come in due course to clarify this question as well.

IX.

ON THE MYSTICAL MARRIAGE OF GOD

God's bride the daughter of a rebel

"The Kingdom of Heaven," says Christ, "is like a king who prepared marriage feasts for his son and invited many to it"

[Mt 22:1ff]. Whom does He mean by "king" if not His Father and God? And for whom did the Father prepare the wedding feasts if not for His Only-Begotten Son, our Lord Jesus Christ? But with whom, with what King, does the Lord and Master of all accept to make an exchange of marriage? Each of us who wants to make a match for his son works hard to find the daughter of someone who is still more noble, glorious, and wealthy than himself. Whom even of equal stature with Himself can God find in order to acquire a bride? For the prophet says concerning Him: "It is He who sits above the circle of the earth, and its inhabitants are as grasshoppers" [Is 40:22]. The same says a little later: "The Lord is the everlasting God, the Creator of the ends of the earth" [Is 40:28] and established their pillars over the abyss. And David says: "Who looks on the earth and it trembles" [Ps 104:32]. Now, given a king so important and so great, where might we look for someone whose daughter could be offered a bride for His Son? Would you like to know whose daughter it is? But my thoughts scatter before the magnitude of His condescension! While I want to say it, I am still terrified by it! However, taking courage from His goodness, I will declare it here: it is the daughter of one who rebelled against Him, one who committed murder and adultery. That is to say, He procures for Himself as a bride the daughter of an adulterer and a murderer.

Have you ever heard of such incomparable and inexpressible goodness and condescension? Have you ever heard of such an excess of love for mankind? Have you ever seen such magnificence of love and goodness? All you who think highly of yourselves, learn from me here to humble yourselves and to moderate your self-opinion, and never to exalt yourselves, be you the mightiest king of kings, or the most noble of nobles, or wealthier than all the other rich men put together. Here you see the Master and Lord of all, the Holy of holies, the blessed God and unique Sovereign, the One Who dwells in unapproachable light, so condescending as to take from a rebel the bride of His only-begotten Son—Who Himself is invisible, unknowable, unsearchable, the Creator and Maker of all—and all of this for your sake and for your salvation! So who is the adulterer and murderer whose daughter God has chosen as a bride for Himself? Why, it is David, Jesse's son, who both slew Urias and committed adultery with his wife. It is David's daughter, I mean Mary the all-undefiled and all-pure virgin, who is brought forth as the bride. I call her all-undefiled and all-pure in relation to us and to the men of the past, comparing her with them and with us, her servants. In relation to her Bridegroom and His Father, however, she is simply human—but still holy, all-holy, and pure and immaculate beyond the people of any generation. This is the one whom God chose and led to marriage with His Son. In what manner? Listen carefully!

The conception of God in the womb of Mary and in the saints

God, the Father of our Lord Jesus Christ, sent down one of His servants, I mean Gabriel the archangel, from the heights of His holy place, to declare to Mary the salutation. The angel descended from above to present the mystery to the virgin, and said to her: "Hail, O favored one, the Lord is with you!" [Lk 1:28]. And, together with the word of greeting, the personal, co-essential, and co-eternal Word of God the Father entered wholly into the womb of the maid, and, by the descent and co-operation of His co-essential Spirit, took on flesh endowed with intelligence and soul from her all-pure blood, and became man. Here, then, is the inexpressible union, and this the mystical marriage, of God, and thus occurred the exchange of God with men. He was united without confusion with our corruptible and wretched nature and essence Who is Himself beyond nature and super-essential. For the Virgin conceived and gave birth paradoxically from two natures—I mean the divinity and the humanity—to one Son, perfect God and perfect man, our Lord Jesus Christ, Who neither abolished her virginity nor was ever separated from the bosom of the Father.

From this point, however, without straying from the word of the Gospel, grace gives me something else to understand and compels me to say it, to speak of that which ever occurs mystically and in all the sons of light. For why did He not say: "He made a wedding feast for his son" instead of "feasts"? It is at this point that I have my new thought. Why? Because for each one of the faithful and sons of light this same marriage is performed in like and scarcely diverging manner. How? In what way? By uniting Himself to us in an all-pure and all-undefiled marriage, God imparts to us something greater than our own powers allow. What is this, then? Listen carefully!

X.

THE SAINTS CONCEIVE IN THEMSELVES THE WORD OF GOD

The Virgin our paradigm, not physically but spiritually

God, the Son of God, entered into the womb of the all-holy Theotokos and, taking flesh from her and becoming man, was born—as we said—perfect God and perfect man. He is the same Who is both without confusion. Now, pay attention! What thing greater has ever happened for us? All of us who believe in the same Son of God and Son of the ever-Virgin Theotokos, Mary, and who, believing, receive the word concerning Him faithfully in our hearts. When we confess Him with our mouths and repent our former lawlessness from the depths of our souls, then immediately—just as God, the Word of the Father, entered into the Virgin's womb—even so do we receive the Word in us, as a kind of seed, while we are being taught the faith. Be amazed on hearing of this dreadful mystery, and welcome this word, worthy of acceptance, with all assurance and faith.

We do not, of course, conceive Him bodily, as did the Virgin and Theotokos, but in a way which is at once spiritual and substantial. And that One Whom the pure Virgin conceived we possess in our hearts, as St Paul says: "God Who called the light to shine from the darkness, has shone in our hearts to give us the light of the knowledge of His Son" [II Cor 4:6]. He as much as says that He has Himself come to be in us substantially. That this is, in fact, the sense of his words he makes clear in the following: "We have this treasure in earthen vessels" [II Cor 4:7], here calling the Holy Spirit the "treasure." Elsewhere he calls the Lord the Spirit: "For the Lord is the Spirit" [II Cor 3:17]. He says these things in order that when you hear the phrase, "Son of God," you should think also of the Spirit, and that you "hear" the latter, too. Similarly, on hearing "Spirit," you should think of the Father with Him, since concerning the Father our Lord says: "God is Spirit" [Jn 4:24]. Everywhere the Apostle teaches the indivisibility and co-essentiality of the Holy Trinity, and that where the Son is, there is the Father also; and where the Father is, there is the Holy Spirit; and where the Holy Spirit is, there is the entire godhead of three Persons, the one God and Father, together with His co-essential Son and Spirit, "Who is blessed forevermore. Amen" [Rom 1:25].

As we have said, therefore, when we believe wholeheartedly and fervently repent, we conceive the Word of God in our hearts, like the Virgin—given, that is, that our souls, too, are virginal and pure. And just as the fire of divinity did not consume her who was all-undefiled, so neither will it burn us up who keep our hearts pure and clean. Instead, that fire comes to us as dew from heaven, and as springs of water unto everlasting life. For proof that we indeed receive ourselves the unbearable flame of divinity, we point to the Lord Who says: "I have come to cast fire upon the earth" [Lk 12:49]. What other fire can He mean than the Spirit co-essential in divinity with Him, together with Whom He enters within us and is beheld there in our heart with the Father? But, since it was once and for all that the Word of God became flesh from the Virgin, and was born, bodily, in manner inexpressible and transcending thought, and, since it is not possible that He should take flesh once more and be born of each of us, what then are we talking about? This: that the same undefiled flesh which He accepted from the pure loins of Mary, the all-pure Theotokos, and with which He was given birth in the body, He gives to us as food. And when we eat of it, when we eat worthily of His flesh, each one of us receives within himself the entirety of God made flesh, our Lord Jesus Christ, Son of God and son of the immaculate Virgin Mary, the very One Who sits at the right hand of God the Father. As He said: "Who eats My flesh and drinks My blood, abides in Me and I in him" [Jn 6:56]. Never does this proceed from us, neither is He born of our bodies and then separated from us. He is no longer among us as an infant, and so known only according to the flesh. Rather, He is present in the body bodilessly, mingled with our essence and nature, and deifying us who share His body, who are become flesh of His flesh and bone of His bone. This is the greater thing which is within us by virtue of His inexpressible economy. This is the mystery all full of holy terror which I hesitate even to write, and tremble in recounting.

Not her equals, but truly her kin

However, since God ever wills that His love for us be unveiled and made manifest so that we, in recognizing His great goodness and doing Him reverence, may love Him the more zealously, so I, moved by the Spirit Who moves and illumines our hearts, have set out to make these mysteries clear to you in writing. I do not do so in order to prove that just any man is the equal of her who gave birth to the Lord in that ineffable engendering. God forbid! This is not possible. One thing is the fleshly begetting of God the Word from her, and another that which spiritually comes to pass in us. On the one hand, she who gave birth to the Son and Word of God made flesh gave birth thus here on earth to the mystery of the re-creation of our race, and to the salvation of the entire world, that re-creation and salvation being our Lord and God, Jesus

Christ. He united in Himself what had been divided [cf. Eph 2:14]
and took away the sin of the world [cf. Jn 1:29]. On the other hand,
the second gives birth in the divine Spirit to the Word of the
knowledge of God, which is ever working in our hearts the
mystery of the renewal of human souls, the communion in and
union with God the Word. The word of Scripture hints at this
second mode of birth: "Through whom we have conceived, and
suffered, and given birth to a spirit of salvation, which we have
brought forth upon the earth" [Is 26:18, LXX]. My intention in
writing is rather that His genuine and infinite love be made
manifest, and that, according to the divine word of our Lord Jesus
Christ, if we desire it, all of us, too, may receive in the manner
described the title of His brothers and become the equals of His
disciples and apostles. Not, indeed, by becoming the latter's
equals in worthiness, nor by accomplishing the missions and
labors which they sustained, but by the action of God's own grace
and gift which He has richly poured out on all who will to believe
in, and to follow Him without turning back. This is just what He
so clearly desires when He says: "My mother and my brothers are
those who hear the word of God and do it" [Lk 8:21].

Do you see how all who hear His word and do it He elevates
to the rank of His mother, and says they are His brothers, and calls
them all His kinsmen? Still, as we said above, she who was His
mother in the body is alone properly so, as she gave birth to Him
ineffably without a man. Yet, all the saints who conceive Him by
grace and gift do possess Him. Thus, while from His immaculate
mother He borrowed her immaculate flesh, and gave her in return
His own divinity—O strange and new exchange!—He takes no
flesh from the saints, but He does make them sharers of His own,
deified flesh. Consider with me, please, the depths of this mystery! While the grace of the Spirit, that is, the flame of the godhead
is of the one Savior and God, from His nature and essence, His
body is not from that source but, on the contrary, is taken from the
all-pure and holy flesh of the Theotokos and from her all-immacu-

late blood. This He took from her and made His own, according to the holy saying: "And the Word became flesh" [Jn 1:14]. As we have said, it is by means of this flesh that He Who is Son of God and son of the Virgin communicates the grace of the Spirit—i.e., of divinity—from, on the one hand, the nature and essence of His co-eternal Father, as He says Himself through His prophet: "And it will come to pass that in those days I will pour out my Spirit upon all flesh" [Jl 2:28], on all flesh, clearly, that believes; and, on the other hand, from the flesh which He took from her who, truly and in the proper sense, gave Him birth.

The new Eve and mother of all and Queen

Just as we all receive of His fulness, so do we all partake of the immaculate flesh of His all-holy Mother which He assumed, and so, just as Christ our God, true God, became her son; even so we, too—O, the ineffable love for mankind!—become sons of His mother, the Theotokos, and brothers of Christ Himself, as through the all-immaculate and ineffable marriage which took place with and in her, the Son of God was born of her and, from Him in turn, all the saints. For just as when Eve received Adam's seed in sexual union and gave birth, and subsequently from and through her all men have been born, so the Theotokos, on receiving the Word of God the Father rather than human seed, conceived and gave birth uniquely to Him Who is the only-begotten of the Father from eternity and, in these last days, is made flesh as the only-begotten of her. While she then ceased from conception and bearing children, her Son both engendered and continues to the present to engender those who believe in Him and keep His holy commandments. It was right that things be done in this way since our generation in incorruption came to pass through the woman, Eve, so our spiritual generation and re-fashioning comes to be through the man, the second Adam, Who is God. Now, notice here that my words are exact: the seed of a man, mortal and corruptible, begets and gives birth through a woman to sons who are mortal and corruptible; the immortal and incorruptible Word of the immortal and incorruptible God, however, begets and gives birth to immortal and incorruptible children, after having first been born of the virgin by the Holy Spirit.

According to this reasoning, therefore, the mother of God is lady and Queen and mistress and mother of all the saints. The saints are all both her servants, since she is the mother of God, and her sons, because they partake of the all-pure flesh of her Son—here is a word worthy of belief [I Tim 1:15], since the flesh of the Lord is the flesh of the Theotokos—and by communing in this same deified flesh of the Lord, we both confess and believe that we partake of life everlasting, provided, of course, that we do not do so unworthily, in which case we do it to our own condemnation. The saints therefore are triply her kin: first, in that they are related to her from the same clay and breath of life [given Adam]; secondly, that they have communion and share with her in the flesh which was taken from her; thirdly and last, that on account of the hallowing which has come to pass in them through her by virtue of the Spirit, each conceives in like manner to her within himself the God of all, as she bore Him in herself. For, if indeed she gave birth to Him in the body, yet she always possessed all of Him in the Spirit, and has Him now, and will ever have Him inseparable from her.

So this is the mystery of the marriages which the Father arranged for His only-begotten Son, Who with Him is co-everlasting and of equal dignity. And He invited many, and sent His servants to invite those who were called to the weddings, and they would not come.

XI.

CALLED TO THE WEDDING FEASTS

Who, then, were those who had been sent? The prophets, He says. Who were those who had been called? The children of the Jews, for they were those who then and from the beginning had been called, and they did not want to listen to them [i.e., the prophets]:

> Again, he sent other servants, saying, "Tell those who are invited, 'Behold, I have made ready my best, my oxen and my fat calves are killed, and everything is ready; come to the marriage feasts.'" But they made light of it and went off, one to his farm, another to his business, while the rest seized his servants, insulted them, and killed them. [Mt 22:4-6]

Whom does He call "servants" here? His apostles. And what is it that He calls His "best"? Clearly, the Kingdom of Heaven which He has prepared from the creation of the world for those who are called according to His plan. What does He mean by His "oxen" and His "fatted calves"? Who else but the virgin's Son, the calf who is "fatted" with divinity. For the Same is truly also in power the unconquerable bull. He has referred to Himself here in the plural because His holy flesh is divided into many portions, in each single one of which He is wholly present. So great, indeed, is His power that He both turns back the enemies of those who receive Him while giving the latter the power to vanquish the world and become, themselves, sons of God. The all-pure Lamb of God is called "lamb" because He is the yearling of the sacrifice [cf. Lev 12:6; Ezek 46:13]. He is the "ram" Who is suspended aloft on the Cross as on two horns, through which He deals a mortal blow to the adversary, and by which He is slain by those who crucify Him. By "other servants," He means His holy apostles whom He sent with the order neither to go out to the gentiles nor to enter the cities of the Samaritans, but instead to go to the lost sheep of the house of Israel. The latter, however, received them not at all. Instead, they insulted and beat some while slaying others, among whom was Stephen, the first of the martyrs. "And on hearing this, the king was angry, and he sent his troops, and destroyed those murderers, and burned their city" [Mt 22:7]. By this, He means the faithless Hebrews whom, indeed, He slaughtered, effecting their entire ruination through the invasion of the Romans. Evil men are called here the "armies of God," who are sent for the punishment of other evil ones, as God says through Moses: "I shall send out against them anger and rage, a mission of evil angels" [Ps 78:49].

> Then he said to his servants, "The wedding feast is ready, but those invited were not worthy. Go therefore to the thoroughfares, and invite to the marriage feast as many as you find." [Mt 22:8-9].

Do you notice the sequence of events? Do you understand the exactness of the parable? For He says "then." Then? When? When the Jews, it is clear, after they had been invited into the Kingdom of Heaven by the apostles and not only could not endure listening to them, but insulted and slew them, our Lord then sent them into all the world and to all the gentiles. So He says:

> And those servants went out into the streets and gathered all whom they found, both bad and good, so the wedding feast was full of guests. [Mt 22:10]

Thus the apostles, when they had gone about the entire inhabited world, proclaimed the word of God and gathered together into one faith of the knowledge of God everyone who would listen, both those who were good and those who were evil in their way of life. The latter, obviously, changed their ways and were led to virtue. This, therefore, is what the "gathered all" means. From what follows we are again taught the same thing:

> But when the king came in to look at the guests, he saw there a man who had no wedding garment; and he said to him, "Friend, how did you get in here without a wedding garment?" And he was speechless. Then the king said to the attendants, "Bind him hand and foot, and cast him into the outer darkness...For many are called, but few are chosen." [Mt 22:11-14]

You see how He says that those who have repented their way

of life are gathered together at the wedding feast. Those, on the other hand, who enter with insincerity or any kind of evil, even if they do make it past the door, are thrown out again by the angels whom He calls here "attendants." The ones who recline at the feast are thus the saints. As for him who has no wedding garment, I understand that some people reckon this to refer only to those who have soiled their own bodies through fornication, or murder, or adultery. This is not at all the case, not at all! Instead, the text signifies all who are stained by any passion or evil whatsoever. And to understand that this is indeed the case, you must listen to St Paul who says:

> Do not be deceived, neither the immoral, nor idolators, nor adulterers, nor sexual perverts, nor thieves, nor the greedy, nor drunkards, nor revilers, nor robbers [and I will add here: neither any who bear malice or envy toward any of their brothers] shall inherit the Kingdom of God. [I Cor 6:9-10]

Nor shall any such have a portion in the joy of our Lord Jesus Christ. Do you see how any wickedness and sin soils the vesture of the soul and causes us to be cast out of the Kingdom?

XII.

ON SEARCHING OUT THE MYSTERIES OF THE KINGDOM OF HEAVEN

Against dabblers and meddlers without experience or faith

Let us therefore put aside every vain and unprofitable disputation, and let us not seek ahead of time to learn what is proper to that hour, i.e., the Second Coming, but instead let us be persuaded by the Master Who says: "Search the Scriptures" [Jn 5:39]. Search, that is, and not meddle! Search the Scriptures and do not busy yourselves with disputes which lie outside the sacred writings. Search the Scriptures so that you may learn about faith, and hope, and love. About faith, so that you may not be tossed about by every wind which comes from the trickery of unstable men, but are rather rooted in the true dogma of the apostolic and catholic Church and "rightly divide" the word of her truth [II Tim 2:15]. And not only this, but you should be taught as well to seek out the fruits of faith and the profit which derives from them through the practice of the commandments. When you have been enabled to find them, then indeed you shall be in possession of hope unashamed, and in the latter you will possess the entirety of love for God. For it is impossible for anyone to possess perfect love for God otherwise than by grace of an unalloyed faith and a hope which is secure and unshakable. Why then do we abandon the examination of ourselves concerning these matters? And, if in fact we have that faith in God which He Himself—Who will judge us—says He will demand of us, why should we busy ourselves with matters which are beyond us, in particular when in truth we fail to see things which lie at our very feet?

Of what sort that faith is which God requires of us, and which we are obliged to have in Him, He Himself makes clear in the Gospels when He says:

> If any man would come after me, let him deny himself and take up his cross, and follow me... [Lk 10:23]

> For whoever comes to me and does not hate his own father and mother and wife and children and brothers and sisters, and in addition his very soul, he cannot be my disciple. [Lk 14:26]

And again: "He who finds his soul"—evidently in what has been said—"shall lose it, and he who shall lose his soul for My sake and the Gospel's"—i.e., in the fulfillment of My commandments—"shall find it in everlasting life" [Mt 10:39]. Did you hear what the identifying marks of faith are? Are you satisfied by these citations, or do you still need to be reminded by what follows from them? Well, if you want to learn that God

requires such a faith from us that we who believe in Him are
not to worry at all about this present life, then learn it precisely
from the Lord Himself, from Him Who says expressly: "Do not
be anxious about tomorrow, what you shall eat or what you
shall drink, or what you shall wear" [Mt 6:25 and 34]. And
leading us up gradually towards what is more perfect, He says:

> If anyone strikes you on the right cheek, turn to him the
> other also; and if anyone would sue you and take your coat,
> let him have your cloak as well. Give to him who begs
> from you, and do not ask for any of it back. [Mt 6:39-40]

Yet more! He goes from one excess of faith to another and
commands us to pray for and love our enemies, to do good to
those who hate us, and to pray for those who abuse us. Still
other things and more He orders us to do of such a kind as to
reveal our faith in Him as coming before all else, and it is only
after this is demonstrated that we can truly call ourselves
believers. For, without these actions, our faith is no faith, dead,
and so, manifestly, are we.

So then, my friend, search yourself most carefully, and if you
should find that none of these things we have spoken about is
lacking in you, but that instead you have done everything to the
last degree with heart aflame and full intention, then you will
certainly perceive yourself as possessing in light that unashamed
hope. It will not be the hope which proceeds from conceit in those
who are perishing, that hope whose vain and deceptive character
none who have it are capable of recognizing, but it will be the
hope which is good and true, and that abides in the light which is
true and unashamed. In this hope you will see love borne aloft as
on the throne of the cherubim, the love which is God. Once you
have found and gazed upon this, from that time forward you will
cease to busy yourself with matters which are invisible and to
come, but you will instead silence others, and command them
neither to meddle nor to inquire into anything concerning things

beyond. For by the very experience of the latter you will have learned that they are all inexpressible in words, and that the mind cannot comprehend them. If meanwhile, however, you have not done what you know a faithful Christian ought chiefly to be doing, but instead have kept faith with the faithless, and by your own conscience are condemned as faithless among the faithful, and no longer have the perfect hope and assurance that you shall be saved, nor are able to say with St Paul:

> I have fought the good fight, I have finished the race, I have kept the faith. Henceforth there is laid up for me the crown of righteousness, which the Lord, the righteous judge, will award to me. [II Tim 4:7-8]

then why do you meddle? Why do you lust to find out whether the saints, when they have attained to the contemplation of God above all and look upon Him, know one another in the Kingdom of Heaven? What is there of any use to you in this? Tell me!

Faith and the commandments are the grammar and tools of transformation

I would really like to hear you tell me what use this is to you! As I said, you are already condemned by your own conscience, since you have not kept the commandments ordered by Christ and on this account have no portion in Him. There is no profit for you at all if you should learn from our teaching what the pleasures and glories and delights and restorations are which are in His Kingdom. On the contrary, you contrive a greater condemnation for yourself because, once having learned about these matters, you hold them in contempt, and want neither to put aside your conceit nor acquire humility.

Now I want to ask you something in all meekness, so please answer me peaceably. If a little child who has not yet learned its letters were to ask someone to interpret the rules of grammar and rhetoric, would anyone who does know put up with it for an instant, or think the child's foolishness worthy of a single word in reply? Would he not instead dismiss the child as foolish and its question as puerile, as asking senselessly after something which exceeds its abilities? And if this is the case, and right and proper concerning matters of grammar, how much the more so is it not true when the issue touches on what transcends words and reason and intellect? Or even if someone were not to learn the basics of grammar yet hear whatever the ancient Greeks wrote in a different vocabulary, and understand that they were speaking the same language as he, there would be nothing wonderful in this, since their words, too, were about perceptible things and their writings vanities piled on vanity.

The matters concerning which you are inquiring, however, are not of such a kind. So, what are they, then? and how so? As the prophet David says: "He bowed the heavens, and came down; thick darkness was under his feet" [Ps 18:10]. What is this "darkness?" It is the flesh itself of the Lord, concerning Whom His forerunner, John, said later: "Whose shoelaces I am unworthy to stoop down and untie" [Mk 1:7]. He descended and came down to us clothed with flesh instead of darkness. And David again:

> He rode upon the cherubim, and flew; He flew upon the
> wings of the wind. And He made darkness His secret place,
> His tabernacle thick clouds dark with water. [Ps 18:10-11]

Do you see how the question is not about things which you can sense, but rather concerns matters divine and incomprehensible, and not easily grasped by everyone? For if He has made darkness and gloom the hiding place of His mysteries, and if one greatly needs the light of the all-Holy Spirit for the comprehension of His hidden mysteries, how, not yet having become yourself the dwelling-place of the divine light, can you attempt to learn of things for which you have not the strength, you who are still imperfect and without the light? Now, in order that you, who sit in darkness, not suppose that He, too, has hidden Himself in darkness, "His tabernacle round about Him," as the prophet David says, learn that that which David calls "tabernacle" is the same as what St Paul names as light: for "He dwells in light unapproach-able" [I Tim 6:16]. Both terms indicate the incomprehensible and unendurable character of His divinity. They do not, though, define the godhead, but as it were set a limit for those who inquire too curiously. You foolish people! Do not suppose that the Lord God on His Ascension entered into and hid Himself in darkness. He instead returns to the same glory of the godhead which fills all things, which is transcendent to everything else, which is His own, and in which He was before His Incarnation. At the same time, He withdraws from us lest we perish utterly. He sets up a darkness which does not veil Himself so much as it protects us: "For our God," Scripture says, "is a fire consuming" not the righteous, but sinners [Dt 4:14].

See to it then! You have just had from us, rather from the Holy Spirit acting through us, a cursory lesson in the divine and dread mysteries of our faith. You have learned that God both came down to earth and ascended again to heaven, that He has made His hiding place, since He will not appear to us with the glory of His Father before the judgment, and that the latter will occur at the time that His Father has, by His own authority, ordained. If then the mysteries of the Kingdom of Heaven are hidden, and if it is not given to anyone to know them, according to the Lord's own word, why, when you have put aside the keeping of His commandments, do you inquire into things which are hidden for everyone? For here you are listening every day to the Apostle shout concerning these same things: "What no eye has seen, nor ear heard, nor the heart of man conceived"—i.e., the good things which "God has prepared for those who love Him" [I Cor 2:9]. Before He ascended and made darkness His hiding place, He gave us His holy commandments as if, we might say, He had given us tools, with faith in Him being as it were a kind of craftsman. So we are the vessels, faith is the worker, the com-mandments the tools through which the Word as Carpenter reforms and re-makes the workers of His commandments, such that through their operation we may be purified and illumined, progressing by grace of the Spirit in the knowledge of the mysteries of the Kingdom of Heaven.

And just as tools without the workmen and the workmen without tools are unable to do anything, just so neither is faith without the fulfillment of the commandments, nor the fulfillment of the commandments without faith able to renew and re-create us, nor make us new men from the old. But, whenever we do possess both within a heart free of doubt, then we shall become the Master's vessels, be made fit for the reception of the spiritual myrrh. Then, too, will He Who makes darkness His hiding-place renew us by the gift of the Holy Spirit and raise us up new instead of old, and part the veil of His darkness and carry our mind away, and allow it to peek as through some narrow opening, and grant it to see Him, still somehow dimly, as one might look on the disk of the sun or moon. It is then that the mind is taught—or, put better—knows and is initiated, and is assured that truly in no other way does one arrive at even partial participation in the ineffable good things of God except by way of the heart's humility, unwavering faith, and the resolve of the whole soul to renounce all the world and everything in it, together with one's own will, in order to keep all of God's commandments. And not only this, but those who believe in Christ, especially those who were baptized in infancy who do not perceive that they have "the gift of God's grace" [Eph 3:7], must all traverse their labors on behalf of virtue, and endure their temptations, without shame—rather, in fact, with joy of heart and with rejoicing.

The reproof of conscience

You, then, who have read this, examine yourself carefully, not with the conceit of knowledge falsely-so-called, nor in the concocting of silly opinions, but with fear and trembling. And if you want to learn what condition your life is in, inquire of your soul and ask it: "Soul, have you kept all of God's commandments, or not?" And, opening the mouth of its conscience, it will tell the whole truth. For it will not seek to please you, rather it will reprove you, and whatever you have stored up and keep in yourself, whether good or ill, it will show you. For within the soul's conscience you will discover whether you have loved the world; whether you have preferred the world to God; whether you have sought the glory of men, or whether you have longed for the glory which is God's gift alone. You will look into yourself as into a chest and will feel around for what is lying at the bottom, and, tossing out the contents one by one, you will know everything clearly. Allow me to suppose the following contents: first of all love of ambition and of vainglory, then the sweetness of human praise, a vesture of hypocrisy, a hidden seed of avarice, and altogether many hidden things, one thing hidden by and on top of another, and right there on top of everything else let us further suppose self-importance—"for knowledge," he says, "puffs up" [I Cor 8:1]—and next to it conceited self-opinion, and the supposition that your puffed-up conceits are really something when, in fact, they are nothing at all. Given that the latter are present, and adding them to all the other articles which we have noted, how can you possibly venture to reflect on the things of God? Surely you must reply: in no way!

The effrontery of the ignorant

So then tell me this as well. If you are not persuaded that a sort of veil covers these things within your heart, but remain instead unconvinced—just like the Hebrews, of whom Paul said the same, i.e., that they do not believe—and if you do not remove this veil from around your heart in order to see the passions which it hides, and so have pity on your wretched soul, and hurry to cleanse it and wash its spiritual eyes and face with hot tears, and throw out behind you all pagan wisdom and knowledge—following the counsel of Paul—so that, by becoming a fool in this world, you may become wise in Christ, then how—tell me!—can I possibly explain to you, who remain a fool, things which concern God and divine matters while the latter remain hidden and invisible? Would you yourself not recognize that I am doing something unworthy, and would you not say to yourself: "This man is truly an idiot! He is trying to explain to me, another fool, things which cannot be seen and are incomprehensible, which transcend everything that breathes beneath the heavens, and every created being above the heavens, too"? For, if even the angels of God do not know when the future things will be, just as they did not know in advance how and in what manner He would appear on earth, neither when nor even that He was going to come down and become man, how much the more ought they to be ignorant of His second coming in glory—when it will be or in what manner—or what He will then share with His saints? St Paul made it clear that this is the truth with respect to the last things when he said: "That the manifold wisdom of God might now be made known to the principalities and powers in the heavenly places" [Eph 3:10]; and the Lord as well, with respect to His parousia, said: "The powers of heaven shall be shaken" [Mt 24:29], instead of saying that they will be startled and amazed when suddenly they see what they had not known at all before. You! If the powers of heaven are ignorant, how do you dare have the nerve to say that the saints will not see one another in the Kingdom of God, then, when they enter into their vision of Him? Or you, you who reply to this and say: "Truly, they must see and know one another"—where did you learn this from?

The knowledge that the blessed will have

O, what ignorance, and madness, and darkness! Don't you shudder? Aren't you afraid? By your own words you shall, both of you, be condemned by the just Judge who is no respecter of persons. To those who say that the saints will neither see nor know one another, but only Him, as supposedly they will be wholly united in all their perceptions to Him alone, He will somehow respond clearly and say: "Have you known Me, O men? Have you seen My light? Have you received Me into yourselves? Have you learned of the energies of My Holy Spirit by experience, or not?" I do not think they will be able to reply and say: "Yes, Lord." For, if they do, He will answer them in return: "How then, if you have come to these things by experience, do you say that those who are going to have Me within themselves will not know one another? I am God Who does not lie; God Who is true; Who is holy, and Who dwells in His saints. How then do I dwell in them? Just as I have said that I am in the Father, and the Father in Me, so also are the saints in Me and I in them; and just as the Father is in Me and I, again, in Him, so too I shall dwell in all the saints, and they shall all abide in Me." In addition, He will also say the following: "If then I am in My saints and My saints are in Me, I in the Father and the Father in Me, and as the Father knows Me even as I know the Father, then clearly the saints, too, know Me and I the saints, and just so ought the saints to be known by and know one another." While this should be obvious even to the insensible, I would like to make it still more clear by insisting yet again that Christ will indwell all the saints.

When therefore the books of each person's conscience shall be opened, in the heart and consciousness of sinners He will find, if nothing else, conceit or vainglory, or heresy, or anger, or envy, or something else of such sins, but if not these, then at least lack of attention, laziness, and not trying with all one's strength to keep God's commandments, and this will reveal a lack of love for Him. On account of this lack then, "Their eyes will be darkened so that they cannot see" [Rom 11:10 = Ps 69:23], and they shall be ashamed, and shall hear: "In as much as you have not done one of the least of My commandments," but have despised it, "you have not done it for me. Depart from me, you cursed, into the eternal fire prepared for the devil and his angels" [Mt 25:41ff]. But, when the books of conscience of the saints are opened—listen well!— Christ Who was hidden in them before will now shine forth, just as He shone forth from the Father before the ages, and the saints shall become like the Highest. Where is this made clear? Listen to the Savior Himself saying: "Then the righteous will shine like the sun" [Mt 13:43]. Now, what time and what sun can He be talking about unless it be in fact that which we have been discussing, and of Himself Who alone is called the sun of righteousness which rises and shines in the righteous alone? And this the beloved disciple, the one who rested his head on Christ's breast, clarifies still more when he says:

> Beloved, we are God's children now; it does not yet appear what we shall be, but we know that when He appears we shall be like Him, for we shall see Him as He is. [I Jn 3:2]

And Paul: "Now I know in part, but then I shall know even as I am known." [I Cor 13:12]

Therefore, if the saints are like God, and if they shall know Him as well as He knows them, as the Father knows the Son and the Son the Father, then the saints ought both to see and to know each other. Indeed, those who have not yet seen one another in the body ought to know each other then. So, how is it that you do not blush at talking, and inquiring, and teaching about matters concerning which you know nothing? For heaven's sake, it is as if you were already enriched by the knowledge of things which are beyond us all, and were appointed beforehand from above as our teachers! Just as the Father is never ignorant of the Son, nor the Son of the Father, just so neither are the saints. They are become gods by adoption through having God indwelling them. They can never be ignorant of each other, but shall look on one another and on each one's glory, like the Son on the Father's glory and the Father on the Son's. What then shall be the glory of the saints? It will be like the Son of God's. The latter Himself points out this very truth most clearly when He says: "The glory which You have given Me I have given to them, that they may be one even as We are one" [Jn 17:22]. Don't you see that the glory given by God the

Father to the Son before the ages is given by the Son Himself to
the saints, so that they all may be one?

The allegory of the prisoner[5]

It therefore follows that they who say that the saints will not
see or even know one another when they are come to the contemplation of God in fact are simply whistling in the dark. Since they
themselves have not arrived at participation in, nor contemplation
nor knowledge of God, they are still chattering about, and giving
testimony to matters which they neither understand nor have ever
seen. It is as if they were saying that the saints on that day, even
as it occurs now, will enter into ecstasy, and so forget both
themselves and those who are with them. It seems to me that their
knowledge of holy Scripture is very weak. They present the
experience of transformation and rapture in the saints of the ages
as the same both now and in the world to come. When they hear
that when such and such a saint arrived at the vision of God, that
his mind was enraptured, that he spent so or so many days and
nights in this condition, remembering nothing earthly at all but
forgetting even his own body along with everything else, and that
he remained welded to the vision and abode there with all his soul
and in all his perceptions, they take this account to mean that
THEN as well (I mean in the Kingdom of God) the saints will
abide in the same condition.[6] They are completely ignorant of the

5 The image of the prisoner owes an obvious debt—though almost
   certainly an indirect one—to Plato's cave-dwellers in the
   Republic: 514-521.
6 Ecstasy as the complete stilling of all mental faculties goes back
   at least to Dionysius the Areopagite (cf., for example, *Mystical
   Theology* I.3 [*PG* 1001A]). Symeon's opponents may also have
   had in mind certain passages from Isaac of Nineveh's *Ascetic
   Homilies* (cf., *Hom.* 23 on "pure prayer," for example, 116-121
   in *The Ascetical Homilies of St Isaac the Syrian* [Boston, 1984]).
   Their argument in sum is that the experience of God is so
   overmastering as to exclude the consciousness of anything

things of the Spirit, and of the invisible God Whose invisible and
incomprehensible mysteries are unknown to those who sit in the
dark, and they are therefore ignorant of the fact that the rapture of
the mind does not apply to the perfect, but to beginners. Think, for
example, of someone who is born and raised in a dark and gloomy
prison cell. In some momentary gleam from a lamp he just begins
to make out, barely, a little something of his room, but remains
ignorant that outside the sun is shining, not to mention everything
else—I mean just this visible world and all the innumerable works
and creations of God. It is exactly thus for the person who lives in
the dark prison of this world's perceptions. When he is illumined
by even the briefest knowledge and begins haltingly to pick out
some small, dim awareness of the mysteries of our faith, he still
remains ignorant in every respect of God's eternal good things,
the inheritance of the saints.

Now, suppose it should happen for the man, sitting for so many
years in his lightless prison, that an opening is made in the roof of his
cell and that he is enabled to see the blue sky. Suppose that little by
little the hole is enlarged so that now he sees a great light such as he
has never seen, nor even imagined could exist. Immediately, he is
seized with amazement, and becomes like someone transported,
keeping his eyes raised toward the light and wondering at what has
suddenly happened to him. It is precisely the same for the person who
has arrived suddenly at the vision of the spiritual light. Just now
liberated from the bonds of the passions and of sensual perceptions,
he is astonished and, for those who do not also perceive the light,

else—indeed, of consciousness itself as we know it. Symeon's
reply that "the rapture of the mind does not apply to the perfect"
seems, on the other hand, borne out by such later accounts as the
famous conversation between Seraphim of Sarov and Nicholas
Motovilov. For the latter, see G. Fedotov, *Treasury of Russian
Spirituality* (Belmont, MA, 1975), 273-279, and for comment,
V. Lossky, *The Mystical Theology of the Eastern Church* (Lon-
don, 1957), 229-231.

seems like someone who has gone out of his mind. He withdraws his whole intellect into himself in wonder at the vision, at the radiance of Him Who is thus revealed to him.

The analogy also holds for what follows. Imagine the first man looking continuously and every day through that hole. The light continues to illumine and reveal more and more, and to widen the gloomy space of his prison. If he continues for a time in this way, he starts to become used to the light, and his original astonishment begins to recede. The same occurs in all of us with respect to the sun. Seeing it has become a habit for us, and we take it for granted. However, if we had never seen it and were one day suddenly to do so, we would cry out with amazement. So, in the same way, when the soul progresses even a little and becomes accustomed to the spiritual light, it leaves behind its original astonishment, and thereupon starts to become aware of something which is both higher and more perfect than its earlier ecstasy.

To continue with the metaphor, the first man comes to learn through the sun's light that he has been confined from birth and lives in a gloomy prison. From that little bit of light, he begins to sense the existence outside of certain wonderful things, but he is unable to reason out or understand what in truth they are. Whenever, though, it happens that he is released from his jail, then he comes to the light together with everything and everyone who dwells within it. Even so, picture with me the one who is now released from the bondage of the body's needs and, for a while, comes to be altogether outside the world and the wretchedness of visible things. Further, picture this whole world as being in fact a dark and lightless prison, and the light of our sun as like that of a little lamp, while outside there lies the inexpressible and ineffable light of the Sun in Three Persons, the light which transcends word and thought and every created light. The things in the world which are lit by that sun are both invisible and unknowable, ineffable and unsearchable, for everyone who inhabits our prison. Yes, there are some people who think that, through the Scriptures, they can understand and see those things. Most of them, though, have no idea whatever that any such experience is possible.

Whenever therefore we seek with all seriousness, with all our faith and longing—not indeed to see the light which lies outside this prison, nor the things which exist in that light and in that world (for no one who ever sought these things was found worthy of seeing them, nor certainly ever will behold them)—but who instead seek first of all to keep the commandments of God, to repent, to grieve, to be humbled, and all the rest of what we talked about above, then indeed something is opened up in us, like a little hole in the visible roof of the heavens, and the light of the world above, immaterial and spiritual, peeks around it. When the soul perceives this, it enters wholly and completely into ecstasy. It becomes all astonishment. It beholds a new wonder, a wonder supremely strange which up to that moment it had never before seen, and in which it abides as it were caught up into heaven and compelled to be present there, and to comprehend it incomprehensibly. In seeing heaven both day and night, the soul is taught from it, and every day learns from it that it is without evening, infinite, and inexpressible. Returning to this prison again the soul no longer desires the world, but longs to see once more that other place and that which it contains.

Ecstasy is only the beginning of glory

Now, you must realize that all this is only an elementary introduction in piety for novices, for those who have stripped themselves for the contest of virtue. Whenever someone perseveres unswervingly toward that vision, not knowing what it is, it is opened to him. And what is opened? Heaven? I do not know. The eye of the heart? Again, I do not know whether to say the one or the other. Yet, by that light and within the house of the soul—I mean clearly this tabernacle of flesh—that wonderful light beyond brightness enters in and lightens him according to the measure which nature allows. And, when he has thus further persevered so that, little by little, he becomes used to the light and lives as if he had always been within it, then, if I may put it so, that which follows may be reckoned as this: he both sees and knows, is initiated into and taught wonders upon wonders, and mysteries upon mysteries, and visions upon visions. And if he were to want to write them all down, there would not be enough paper nor ink to suffice him. I think that he would lack the time even to tell of these things in any detail. Indeed, how could he in any case write down what cannot be spoken, but which is entirely inexpressible and ineffable? Now, as in the light or—better—as united with it, and as no longer in ecstasy, he instead comes to perceive himself and what is his own. He sees his neighbors as they are in their own right. He knows and predicts that, when he comes to depart this prison and, in particular, after the general resurrection, he will also look upon that unwavering light as it is, and that all the good things within it "which no eye has seen, nor ear heard, nor the heart of man conceived, what God has prepared for those who love Him" [I Cor 2:9], will be revealed to him the more clearly through the same light within him now and by which he is illumined. We shall not be deprived THEN of knowing or seeing, but, as we have demonstrated above, according to the measure which each has of the radiance and vision of the light, both the knowledge and vision of God, and the recognition and knowledge of one another shall grow ever greater and more clear in joy inexpressible and rejoicing forever and ever. Both the prophets of the Old Testament and many of the saints of the New have witnessed to this in their deeds, calling by name those whom they had never seen, and recognizing indeed those whom they had never known before.

Rebuke and exhortation

Those who say therefore that the saints neither know nor see one another, let them rather be persuaded—assuming they would listen to me—not to go inquiring into matters which are incomprehensible, and let them not cease instead from attending to and examining themselves. You who ignore everything we have been saying, and who have not arrived yourselves at the perception and knowledge and experience of divine illumination and contemplation, how can you talk or write at all about such things without shuddering? For, if we are obliged to render an account for every idle word, how much the more shall we not be tried and convicted as vain babblers when our words touch on matters such as these? And vain babble is not, as some might suppose, just unedifying talk. It also applies to talk which is unsupported by practice and the knowledge won from experience. If I do not despise the glory of this world and hold it in contempt with all my soul as injurious to the soul and as depriving me of heaven's glory, and then if I should teach others about the latter and encourage them to abstain from it, will not my words be vain and idle and empty? Shall I not be condemned as a liar? Again, if I do not receive the grace of the Spirit perceptibly and consciously, nor through Him become one who is taught by God, nor receive a word of wisdom and knowledge from on high, yet still set off shamelessly to interpret the God-inspired Scriptures and set myself up in the position of a teacher, plainly depending on false knowledge for this authority, will then God allow me to escape without examination and not demand an accounting from me? Certainly not! If you will listen, then learn what is exalted and divine even from what is base and human. Tell me, what man, even if he were wondered at as beyond everyone in his wisdom and knowledge and understanding of the laws, and if he were decked out with righteousness and piety, would dare sit down as a judge with judges without an imperial appointment, and call himself a judge, and legislate for others? If he were to do this, would the emperor not depose him and punish him according to the full rigor of the law?[7] O, the shamelessness!

7 This passage marks the first of many appearances of the figure of the emperor. Symeon's own background at the imperial court, as well as his general experience as an inhabitant of early eleventh-

No one dares hold the earthly king in contempt and seize rank and honor from him in order to assign them to himself. And you! Do you dare hold the Heavenly King in contempt, like a nobody, and lay hands on the apostolic rank without His influence and consent? And since you are behaving in just this way, do you fancy that the Master will let it pass without trial? Certainly not, never!

But You, O Lord, grant us to know You and rightly fear You, and to abide in Your holy will. I beg you, brothers, cease and desist from these inquiries. Make haste instead by grace of repentance and tears and humility, and by fulfillment of all of the commandments, to purify your own souls "from every stain of flesh and spirit" [II Cor 7:1], so that you may enjoy both the present and the future good things in a state of revelation, of perception and of vision, through the grace and love for humanity of our Lord Jesus Christ, to whom be glory, honor, and worship, together with the Father and the Holy Spirit, now and ever, and unto ages of ages. Amen.

---

century Constantinople, is much in evidence. The presence of the sovereign in the royal box at the capital's Hippodrome (site of chariot races and other sporting events) in *Discourse* II below (pp. 91-92) is something that would have been familiar to any of the city's inhabitants.

SECOND ETHICAL DISCOURSE

Introduction

Discourse II, divided into seven chapters, expands on the theme of predestination. God, Symeon argues, indeed knew from before the world who would make up the company of saints in the new creation, but this foreknowledge in no way implies that He willed some to be saved and others damned. Rather, he insists in the first chapter, human free will is a constant, and to plead predestination against moving to repentance and ascetic effort is merely an excuse for sloth. Instead, as his long argument in the remaining chapters seeks to demonstrate, God prepared the salvation of the world from the beginning and that salvation awaits each person "before the gates" of his or her own heart. In chapters two through six, he rehearses the history of God's saving activity, drawing a connection from the creation of Eve, taken from Adam's side, through the election of Israel to the birth of Christ from Mary. Playing on the scriptural notions of "remnant" and "portion," he traces a succession of stages in the realization of God's hidden intention of universal salvation. Throughout the sacred history from Adam through Noah, Abraham and Moses to the Theotokos and Christ, it is the one and unique "portion," originally taken from the first man, whose story is being told, and whose purpose is finally disclosed in the chosen vessel, Mary the Virgin, through whom the Incarnation of the Word takes place. It is the same flesh, Adam's, which is deified by the risen Christ and in which thus the original man is renewed together with his descendants and the entire world. In his concluding chapter Symeon returns to the theme of the first discourse. The new paradise and divinized creation is present now in the Church, the body of Christ, and it is become available to everyone. Whoever wills to do so has only to knock and enter. We have only to appropriate through faith and faith's corollary, the freely-willed taking up of Christ's cross, what God has already accomplished in His Son. The treasures of heaven, of the Holy Spirit, await our choice.

I.

ON THE SAYING "THOSE WHOM HE FOREKNEW, THE SAME HE ALSO PREDESTINED"[1]

"Predestination" is an excuse for sloth: God calls everyone to repentance

I have heard many people say: "Because the Apostle says; 'Those whom God foreknew, the same He also predestined; and those whom He predestined, He also called; and those whom He called, the same also glorified' [Rom 8:29-30] what good is it to me if I throw myself into many labors, if I give proof of repentance and conversion, when I am neither foreknown nor predestined by God to be saved and conformed to the glory of God His Son?" We are naturally obliged to state our opinion clearly to such people, and to reply: O, you! Why do you reason to your own perdition rather than your salvation? And why do you pick out for yourselves the obscure passages of inspired Scripture and then tear them out of context and twist

1 This marks the beginning of Symeon's discussion of Rom 8:29-30 against the argument of some of his opponents on behalf of the doctrine—or at least, the opinion—of predestination. As evident from the following, the New Theologian abhors this notion. His reply is based both on the obvious objection that predestination makes nonsense of God's justice and of His insistent calls for our repentance—why ask us to do anything when the issue has been decided by the divine will from before the world?—and on two other points. First, God's will and His foreknowledge are somehow to be distinguished. This distinction rests, secondly, on the mysterious quality of human freedom. As made according to the divine image, every human soul is endowed with an inalienable freedom of action (the *autexousion* in the patristic language), and this capacity remains in us even after the Fall. Further, even God Himself will not presume to bruise or force this freedom. Here Symeon is echoing a long-established theme in the Greek Christian tradition (cf. Meyendorff, *Byzantine Theology*, 139-146).

them in order to accomplish your own destruction? Do you not hear the Savior crying out every day: "As I live...I have no pleasure in the death of the wicked, but that the wicked turn from his way and live" [Ezek 33:11]? Do you not hear Him Who says: "Repent, for the Kingdom of Heaven is at hand" [Mt 3:2]; and again: "Just so, I tell you, there is joy in heaven over one sinner who repents" [Lk 15:7, adapted]? Did He ever say to some: "Do not repent for I will not accept you," while to others who were predestined: "But you, repent! because I knew you beforehand"? Of course not! Instead, throughout the world and in every church He shouts: "Come to Me, all who labor and are heavy laden, and I will give you rest" [Mt 11:28]. Come, He says, all you who are burdened with many sins, to the One Who takes away the sin of the world; come, all who thirst, to the fountain which flows forever and never dies.

Does He distinguish and separate anyone out, calling one to Himself as foreknown while sending the other away as not pre-destined? Never! Therefore, "you should not make excuses for your sins" [Ps 140:4, LXX], nor should you want to make the Apostle's words an occasion for your own destruction, but should run, all of you, to the Master Who calls you. For even if someone is a publican, or a fornicator, an adulterer, a murderer, or whatever else, the Master does not turn him away, but takes away the burden of his sins immediately and makes him free. And how does He take away the other's burden? Just as He once took away that of the paralytic when He said to the latter: "My son, your sins are forgiven" [Mt 9:2], and the man was immediately relieved of his burden and, in addition, received the cure of his body. So then, let everyone who wants approach Him, and let the one shout: "Son of David, have mercy on me"; and, if he hears, "What do you want Me to do for you?" let him say quickly, "Lord, let me receive my sight," and right away he will hear, "So I desire. Receive your sight" [Lk 18:38-42]. Let another say, "Lord, my daughter"—i.e., my soul—"is severely possessed by a demon" [Mt 15:22], and he will hear: "I will come to heal her" [Mt 8:7]. If someone is hesitant and does not wish to approach the Master, even if He comes to him and says, "Follow Me" [Mt 9:9], then let him follow Him as the publican once did, abandoning his counting tables and his avarice, and, I am sure, He shall make of him, too, an evangelist rather than a tax collector. If someone else is a paralytic, lying for years in sloth, carelessness, and love of pleasure, and if he should see another, be it the Master Himself or one of His disciples, come to him and ask, "Do you want to be healed?" [Jn 5:2-7], let him receive the word joyfully and reply immediately: "Yes, Lord, but I have no man to put me into the pool of repentance." And then if he should hear, "Rise, take up your bed, and follow me," let him get up right away and run after the footsteps of the One Who has called him from on high.

Now, if someone does not wish, whether like the sinful woman to embrace the feet of Christ [Lk 7:38], or like the prodigal son to run back to Him with burning repentance [Lk 15:11ff], or like the woman with a hemorrhage and bowed with infirmity [Lk 8:43 and 13:11] even to approach Him, why does he then make excuses for his sins by saying, "Those whom He foreknew, them also"—and them alone!—"He called"? One may perhaps reasonably reply to the person so disposed that "God, Who is before eternity and Who knows all things before creating them, also knew *you* beforehand, knew that you would not obey Him when He called, that you would not believe in His promises and in His words, yet still, even while knowing this, He "bowed the heavens and came down" [Ps 18:19] and became man, and for your sake has come to the place where you lie prone. Indeed, visiting you many times every day, sometimes in His own Person and sometimes as well through His servants, He exhorts you to get up from the calamity in which you lie and to follow Him Who ascends to the Kingdom of Heaven and enter it together with Him. But you, you still refuse to do it. Then tell me, who is responsible for your perdition and disobedience? You, who refuse to obey and who will not follow your Master, or God Himself Who made you, Who knew beforehand that you would not obey Him, but would instead abide in your hardened and impenitent heart? I think that you will certainly say, "He is not responsible, but I am myself," because God's forbearance is not the cause of our hardness. Rather, it is our own lack of compliance.

Example of the emperor and the arena: God is foreknowledge

For God knows all things beforehand, both past and present at once, and everything which is going to happen in the future up to the end of world. He sees them as already present, because in and through Him all things hold together [Col 1:17]. Indeed, just as today the emperor takes in with a glance those who race and who wrestle in the arena, but does not thereby make himself responsible for the victory of the winners or the failure of the losers—the zeal, or in other cases the slackness, of the contestants being cause of their victory or defeat—understand with me that it is just so with God Himself. When He endowed us with free will, giving commandments to teach us instead how we must oppose our adversaries, He left it to the free choice of each either to oppose and vanquish the enemy, or to relax and be miserably defeated by him. Nor does He leave us entirely to ourselves—for He knows the weakness of human nature—but rather is present Himself with us and, indeed, allies Himself with those who choose to struggle, and mysteriously imbues us with strength, and Himself, not we, accomplishes the victory over the adversary. This the earthly emperor is unable to do, since he is himself also a man, and is rather in need himself of assistance, just as we require it, too.

God, on the other hand, Who is mighty and invincible, becomes, as we just said, an ally of those who willingly choose to do battle with the enemy, and He establishes them as victors over the cunning of the devil. He does not, however, compel any who do not so choose to this war, in order that He not destroy the power of choice which is proper to our reasoning nature, made according to His own image, and bring us down to the level of unreasoning brutes. Thus God, as we have explained, sees us all at once as if in an arena, just like the earthly emperor looks down on the athletes in competition. But, while the latter does not know who will lose and who will win until he sees the outcome of their contest and, though he may prepare the victors' crowns beforehand, he still does not know to whom he is going to present them; the King of Heaven, on the other hand, knows from before the ages exactly who the victors and vanquished are going to be. This is why He said to those who asked Him if they could sit at His right hand and His left in His glory: "It is not mine to give to you" [Mt 20:23], but that it will be given instead to those for whom it was prepared.

God does not compel

This is therefore what Paul himself also knew when he said rightly:

> Those whom God foreknew, the same He also predestined; and those whom He predestined, He also called; and those whom He called, the same He also glorified. [Rom 8:29-30]

It is not God's foreknowledge of those who, by their free choice and zeal, will prevail which is the cause of their victory, just as, again, it is not His knowing beforehand who will fall and be vanquished which is responsible for their defeat. Instead, it is the zeal, deliberate choice, and courage of each of us which effects the victory. Our faithlessness and sloth, our irresolution and indolence, on the other hand, comprise our defeat and perdition. So, while reclining on our bed of worldly affection and love of pleasure, let us not say: "Those whom God fore-knew, them also He predestined," without perceiving just what it is we are saying. Yes, indeed, He truly knew you beforehand as inattentive and disobedient and lazy, but this is certainly not because He ordered or foreordained it that you should have no power to repent yourself nor, if you will it, to get up and obey. You, though, when you say this, are clearly calling God a liar. While He says, "I came not to call the righteous but sinners to repentance" [Mt 9:13], *you*, lazy and unwilling to turn around and repent of your evil, contradict Him, as it were, and call Him a liar Who never lies, when you make such excuses as these. "Those who are going to repent", you say, "were predestined, but I am not one of them. So, let them repent therefore whom God clearly foreknew, and whom He also predestined." O what a lack of feeling! O shamelessness of soul and worse than the demons themselves! When did anyone ever hear of one of them saying such a thing? Where was it ever heard that a demon blamed God for its own damnation? Let us then not blame the demons, for here there is a human soul which thinks up blasphemies even worse than theirs.

So tell me, where did you learn that you did not belong to those who are foreknown and predestined to become conformed to the image of God's glory? Tell me, who told you this? Was it, maybe, God Who announced this to you, Himself, or by one of His prophets, or through an angel? "No," you say, "but I do suppose that I am not predestined to salvation, and that all my effort would be in vain." And why do you not believe instead with all your soul that God has sent His only-begotten Son on the earth for your sake alone, and for your salvation, that He knew you beforehand and predestined you to become His brother and co-heir? Why are you not eager to love Him with all your heart and to honor His saving commandments? Why do you not rather believe that, having been slaughtered for your sake, He will never abandon you, nor allow you to perish? Do you not hear Him saying: "Can a woman forget her sucking child...yet I will not forget you" [Is 49:15]? So, if by anticipation you judge yourself unworthy, and willfully separate yourself from the flock of

Christ's sheep, you should understand that it is none other than you who are the cause of your own damnation.

Therefore, casting out of our souls all faithlessness, sloth, and hesitation, let us draw near with all our heart, with unhesitating faith and burning desire, like slaves who have been newly purchased with precious blood. Indeed, with reverence for the price paid on our behalf, and with love for our Master Who paid it, and as having accepted His love for us, let us recognize that, if He had not wished to save by means of Himself us who have been purchased, He would not have come down to earth, nor would He have been slain for our sake. But, as it is written, He has done this because He wills that all should be saved. Listen to Him say it Himself: "I did not come to judge the world, but to save the world" [Jn 12:17].

However, let us now turn back to the question before us.

II.

ALL WHO HAVE BEEN BAPTIZED INTO CHRIST ARE FOREKNOWN AND PREDESTINED BY GOD

The preceding argument has certainly established this clearly. We must, however, go on to speak about the meaning of these sayings, the depth of knowledge in the Apostle's words and thoughts, so that you learn thereby that all who have believed in Christ, both monks and lay people, are foreknown and predestined, and become conformed to the image of the Son of God. Nor this alone, but also that all of them, as predestined, are called; and, as called, they are also justified; and, as justified, they are glorified. Because, while those perish who, after being baptized and believing in Christ, and becoming conformed to the image of the Son of God, do not keep themselves in this state, all who abide in it are saved. But here I begin the theme of the discourse and will start where it is best to begin, at the beginning.

The Scripture says:

When the Most High divided up the nations, the sons of
Adam whom He had dispersed, He fixed the bounds of the
peoples according to the number of the angels of God. For
the Lord's portion is His people, and Israel His allotted
heritage. [Dt 32:8-9]

What is meant by this is the following: God divided up all the
nations. What nations are these? The very sons of Adam. If
then, all are sons of Adam, how does Scripture call them
nations? Because, just as Adam was immortal before transgressing God's commandment, and incorrupt, a fellow-citizen
and one who conversed with the angels, and, from the moment
he transgressed God's commandment, fell away from all these
good things and was cast out of Paradise, and became thus
mortal and corruptible, so, too, are all who have been begotten
of him. For they multiplied and, falling into an ignorance of
God like the one who said: "I will set my throne above the
clouds and I will make myself like the Most High" [Is 14:13-
14], they, too, thought wickedly and began to build a tower and
tried to climb up to heaven. For this reason, by way of a curse
and punishment, He confused their languages and cut off their
agreement in wickedness. It is as if He cut limbs off from the
body of Adam, separating and scattering them away from him
and each other. To each limb He gave a separate language so
that never again would they be able to join together. This is
therefore why He does not call them "men," but "nations"
[pagans, gentiles].

God's portion: the predestined salvation from Adam's rib
   to Christ

When He had thus scattered them throughout all the earth, He
assigned an angel guardian to each portion. Now, consider with
me exactly how all things are foreknown by God and predestined
from the beginning of the world and of the ages. For, because He

had fore-ordained their re-creation in a new birth, God, when He took the one portion, the rib, from the one body of Adam and, after He replaced the part taken with flesh, He built up the rib into a woman, just so, after borrowing this portion from Adam's body and replacing it with other flesh, what He had borrowed became His portion and was no longer reckoned as belonging to Adam's body. Instead, it was the Lord's portion, outside Adam's body, although it had been taken from him and was akin to him. Therefore, He did not assign an angel as guardian of this portion but, in the manner of a tutor for a son or like a general for a people or an army, He gave them the Archangel Michael. God, however, remained their protector and overseer, and so He called them "Israel," that is, the intellect which contemplates God.[2] So, too, Christ is said to have been born of the daughter of Adam and of David. Thus the same portion, I mean that taken from the body of Adam, is what is intended by St Matthew's genealogy [cf. Mt 1:1ff] and not the whole body [of Adam], since Adam as a whole fell from the divine glory.

How is this so, and why? It is in order that, just as the portion was taken from the whole body of Adam and built up into a woman, so, in turn, the same portion set aside from the woman should be built up into a man and become a new Adam, our Lord Jesus Christ. This is the portion which St Paul called the "chosen remnant" [Rom 11:5]. Thus, as it was from the portion set apart, the woman herself, that the curse spread to the whole body, that is, the human race, so in turn is it by the same part set aside, I mean the Lord's body, that the blessing is diffused throughout all humanity. It is for this reason that He also descended to hell, so that His manifestation and salvation might come to all the saints who were before His appearance, and so that He could join all who had fallen asleep from the beginning with all who are going to

2 Cf. *SC* 122, 330, note 1, on the history of this interpretation of "Israel," dating back to Philo.

become saints up to the end of the world. Thus He was also laid in the tomb, in order, by the death of His own body, to make all bodies which have died partakers of the everlasting Resurrection. Therefore Israel, which had become God's inheritance and bore the title of His portion, He rightly called His vineyard. He set a fence around it, as around another Paradise, from which Adam was cast out yet again, I mean the race which is from his body, that is, the gentiles. And while the angel, instead of the sword of fire was guarding it in order to keep the gentiles from entering, it was God Who was the gardener.

Therefore just like Eve, she who was the portion of the whole body of Adam, was first to speak to the serpent, first to reveal to it what God had commanded, and first, after accepting what the serpent had sowed in her, to eat from the tree—Adam not being present—and then later ministered to the man by giving him to eat as well from it, so yet later did the same occur with Israel. Because, just as she had done, so did Israel put aside faith and love for the God Who had chosen him out of all the nations, abandon His worship, and offer libations and sacrifices to idols, and ate and drank of them. God then, knowing this beforehand—since He is God and knows all things—took again from the same part set aside, I mean from the side of Adam, and preserved it for Himself as His portion, His "lot," from the tribe of Judah. And, because all the rest were bound up together in faithlessness, He took His part set aside and built it up into a woman, I mean Mary the all-unde-filed. Then, possessing in Himself, as a seed of the faith in God, the flesh assumed from the holy Theotokos and Ever-Virgin Mary, the most holy God built for Himself a temple, became Himself the God-Man. Now, since this flesh which He assumed from the pure Theotokos was not of the woman, but was built up within a woman from Adam, Christ is said to bear Adam, and He becomes a second Adam taken from the first, and is called this by Scripture [cf. I Cor 15:48-49]. He is Son of God and son, not of the woman but of Adam. Where is this written? It says so in the

Gospel of St Luke. Look it up, if you like, and you will find His genealogy given in just this manner. For, when the Gospel says that He was "supposed" a son of Joseph, it adds: "the son of Eli, the son of Matthan..." and, continuing on through the line of descent of the portion reserved, says finally: "son of Enos, the son of Seth, the son of Adam, the son of God" [Lk 3:23-38]. Going up from Joseph to Adam step by step, he does not recall the woman at all, but leaves the matter wholly in mystery.

Israel a second Paradise, and Abraham's faith the Tree of Life

As we said, God took this portion set aside, as bearing within itself the seed of faith, and became man. The whole Adam, which is to say all his race which had been removed from the portion reserved and, as it were, cast out of the new Paradise, out of the Lord's part and His vineyard, God decided to justify through the seed of faith, by faith in Himself, just as He had promised to Abraham. He did not, however, decide on this plan at the time that Abraham demonstrated his faith by sacrificing Isaac—as some too clever people might fancy. Instead, knowing all this from before the foundation of the world, and having predestined that the portion reserved, and all who of the portion freely chose faith in it after having begun to separate themselves from it, should be saved by faith, He then revealed His will predestined from of old to Abraham after the latter had, as it were, shown himself faithful. On hearing this, we might think that, because Abraham believed in God Who said: "In you shall the nations be blessed" [Gen 22:18], we have received on account of him the same blessing and adoption to sonship by faith, wrongly imagining this promise given us to be a kind of acknowledgment of Abraham's faith, and not instead as predestined by God's ineffable economy before the ages and now, by faith, promised and revealed to us in Abraham. No, it is not so, not at all! For, when this part set aside [i.e., Israel] among the apportioning of the sons of Adam, the gentiles, became

the Lord's portion according to Scripture, He planted it as a kind
of second Paradise with the tree of life in its midst, that is to say,
faith in God and in God's Spirit. But, since this portion was from
Adam's side and had been made into a woman, and the woman
was first to transgress, and because God knew beforehand that
neither would this [new] portion in its turn keep faith with Him,
when before the ages He knew this, then He was pleased to recall
all the nations which had been rejected and shut out of this portion,
and had become estranged from it, and bring them back again to
be added and united to the portion taken from the first.

Christ, the son of Adam and redemption of the Gentiles

Now pay careful attention to what I am saying, because the
concept here is difficult to understand. When the Jewish people,
which was called Israel (for this is the portion which is from the
man's side), transgressed the commandment given to it by God—
"Hear O Israel," He says, "the Lord your God is One Lord" [Dt
6:4]—when it had transgressed this and worshipped demons, and
bowed to idols, and had eaten of their libations and sacrifices, then
from it in turn as from a single body of what had been built up out
of many members into one people, God took His own portion and
preserved it unmingled for Himself. The remaining body, however, the part which had been broken off from this portion and had
inclined toward idolatry, God banished and drove out of Paradise,
that is, out of the vineyard of His portion. Then, from that which
was His part through faith according to election, which was itself
taken from Adam's side, as it were taking for Himself a kind of
little seed, God the Word became man. This is to say, I repeat, that
the second Adam is son of the first as born from his side without
intercourse or emission of seed, and it is thus that the whole body
of the first Adam and all his members are blessed. We mean that
the people of the gentiles who had formerly been cast out are now,
through Adam's son the God-Man, united by faith to the portion
reserved from Adam's side.

This is therefore what the divine Paul says was known and predestined before the ages by the God Who knows all things in advance: that all the nations from east to west are invited and, as many as believe, are joined to Him Who has become flesh from the side of their father, to Christ, the Son of God and son of Adam. So shall the two become one [Eph 2:14], one body with Christ, His co-participants, brothers, and co-heirs with Him. Indeed, they become Christ Himself, Who thus comprises the nations which had been turned out and scattered abroad. As many, though, as do not believe remain outside together with those who were removed from the portion of faith. I mean here the Jews, who were cast out and rejected because of their unbelief. For those who listen closely, this is also clear from the words of the Gospel:

> All authority in heaven and on earth has been given to Me.
> Go into all the world and preach the Gospel of the King-
> dom. He who believes and is baptized shall be saved, but
> he who does not believe will be condemned. [Mt 28:18 and
> Mk 16:15-16]

But let us take the matter up again and go through what we said above in brief in order that our point may this time be seen the more easily by everyone.

III.

RECAPITULATION OF WHAT WAS SAID IN THE FIRST DISCOURSE

The Garden and the seven days of creation

So, God made heaven and earth and everything in them—that we may look again into the hidden thoughts of Scripture—and then, afterwards, He made man according to His image and likeness, that is, Adam alone. He did all this in six days and on the seventh He rested, doing nothing on that day nor calling the first day the eighth, in order that the days of the week be called seven only, and not eight, and so that turning always back on themselves they should comprise the number of the weeks. For in these seven days the Creator may be seen foreshadowing the *seven ages*.[3] Then, when the Master of all had completed all these things, since He had foreseen as God that the man would transgress His commandment and remain impenitent, and since it was entirely necessary that as impenitent he should be punished and condemned, He did not permit him to remain in the world which He had created in the six days but, after resting on the seventh day and following that day's completion, then He afterwards planted the garden in the East.

In what manner and why did He do this? So that far from this world the man might be introduced, like a sort of king, into something like a palace or a resplendent city, and this in order that, on transgressing God's commandment and therefore falling away from the Kingdom and being cast out of the royal residence into exile, he could be condemned yet live on in this world with hope. For, if God had not arranged matters in this way, but instead had left this world the only one and had placed man within it [from the beginning], where would He have been able to exile the man after the latter had transgressed without either confessing his fault or repenting it? Where could Adam have gone to live, die, and return again to the earth from which he had been taken? Clearly, nowhere at all. Instead, he would have had to have been condemned alive to hell without any hope from that time on for any restoration to salvation, and thus [there would have been] no begetting and growth of mankind into a multitude, and that great and magnificent work of God's wisdom which is mankind would have perished utterly.

The Eighth Day: God's provision for the Fall and Redemption

However, because God knew before the ages that Adam was

---

3 See above, *Discourse* I.1, page 25, note 2.

going to transgress, and since He had predestined the man's re-creation by a new birth, for this reason, after He had made all things, and had rested, and had mystically prefigured both the times and the ages in the seven days, He afterwards took the pledges of the new creation like a sort of leaven and seed, a portion of each of His works which had been created during the seven days, and placed them not in the seventh, but in the eighth day. Thus He signified the age to come beforehand by His creation on the eighth day. He did not number this day with the seven, nor did He make it manifest, but allowed it rather to remain wholly unknown to those who were before the Law, and then revealed it, though still obscurely, to the prophets of the Law who announced it. To those of us who believe, however, who await the unsetting sun of righteousness which has not yet risen, He has made it plain as the light of dawn. Now then, I said that God took portions: from all the earth He took one spot in which He planted the garden; from the whole body of Adam one rib, a single member; but from the seven days He took nothing. How is this? Because, while those portions were taken in order that what is co-natural and akin to them should be renewed and united to the heavenly beings, the days, on the other hand, were left aside in that they are not going to be renewed, but on that day will be made to cease entirely. God did not therefore take a portion for renewal from them, but He did from the seven ages. How? Listen!

Seven ages must be fulfilled according to the number of the seven days. Six of them have already gone by while the seventh is not yet finished, but from the latter God takes a portion and joins it to the age which is everlasting and without end. As for how much He foreordained to take, or when the end of these days will take place, no one knows except the Holy Trinity, the one and indivisible Godhead. The saying of the Savior, Jesus Christ, that the Son knows neither the day nor the hour [cf. Mt 24:36], was said according to the ignorance of His humanity, not of His divinity. Why did He not take a portion from the days, but did from the ages? Because, while the ages are measured by days and weeks and are thus called ages, the future and everlasting age is not measured by days, but both is and shall be immeasurable and without end. Thus, in that there shall be no days but instead a single age, so did God take no portion from the days but did so from the ages, in order to unite that portion to the age to come. Now, the portion taken from the earth was clearly Paradise, a type of the Heavenly Jerusalem—I mean, obviously, of the Kingdom of Heaven—in which God placed the man so that he could be led progressively upwards from the type and shadow to the truth. The tree of life in the middle of Paradise was an image of the everlasting life which is God Himself. Adam's rib, which was built up into the woman, was a type of the Church, yet another mystery of the economy of salvation. Thus, when man fell away from the image which had been created as a type of the Kingdom of Heaven, that is, from Paradise, and away from the tree of life, he could still be joined through the rib to Christ and to God, and be led up again to that ancient and primordial beauty.

Because Eve was first deceived and transgressed the commandment, and ate of the fruit, and then gave it to Adam who ate it in turn, and because neither wished in any way to repent and fall down before the Master, they were exiled from there and condemned to make their home in this world. But, note as well the inexpressible goodness of God's Providence with regard to man. For, once he had been brought down by sin to corruption, in order that he not become immortal by eating of the tree of life—since he would have become thereby both corruptible and immortal, and sin would thus have become immortal as well—God ordained the fiery sword to guard the entrance to the tree of life.

IV.

ON THE FLOOD AND THE CONTENTS OF THE ARK

The first pair knew each other and bore children, and they

raised up sons and daughters, and Adam "called his wife's name 'Eve,' because she was the mother of all living" [Gen 3:20]. But, when men had multiplied and fallen into an abyss of evil and a great multitude of sins, God set about to wash clean the world with water and to wipe man off the face of the earth. At the same time, He did not abandon His portion. Rather, He preserved Noah and his sons and daughters on the ark. Again, the ark was a type of the Theotokos and Noah of Christ, and the men with Noah were a first-fruit of the portion of the Jews, of those who would believe in Christ, while the wild beasts and the animals and birds and reptiles constituted a type of the gentiles. Thus accordingly, if the ark after the flood contained Noah, and Mary the Theotokos contained the Incarnate One, God and man, yet the ark saved only Noah and those who were with him, while Christ, on the other hand, delivered both His "ark" and all the world from the flood of sin, from the slavery of the Law, and from death.

After the flood, though, men were once again brought down to ignorance of God and, at the same time, once more became stiff-necked and haughty because they were of one mouth, that is, had a single language and the same words. So they began to build a tower and tried to climb up into heaven, imagining within themselves—yet again!—that they were God's equals [Gen 11:1ff]. When God therefore was about to confuse their languages and thus divide and scatter them throughout the earth—since they had become many members from Adam's side yet were one body thanks to their single language—He once again took from them a portion for Himself, that is, the "rib," and then, when He had turned the remaining body into many portions of members, He scattered them and called them, who were wholly ignorant of Him, "gentiles." His own portion He named "Israel," which means "the one who sees God." This was Abraham, in whom the seed of faith and of the knowledge of God was preserved thenceforth by hereditary succession, and to whom God appeared and said: "Go forth from your country and your kindred...to the land that I will show you" [Gen 12:1]. To Abraham also He gave the circumcision, revealing it to him as a kind of sign and seal. Further, He swore to him that his seed would be multiplied like the stars in heaven and like the sand which lines the seashore. After this, God appeared again to him and said: "Know of a surety that your descendants will be sojourners in a land that is not yours" [Gen 15:13], informing him beforetime of Joseph's descent into Egypt together with his father, Jacob, and his brothers. From the latter the portion would multiply and become a great nation whom God, through Moses, would lead out of Egypt, feasting them beforehand with the lamb which was the antitype of the true Lamb. Then, after He had both parted the sea and led them across, and had brought them through the desert while feeding them there for forty years, they became "the Lord's portion, His people Jacob, Israel His allotted inheritance." [Dt 32:9, LXX]

They had thus the circumcision as a seal, and all were circumcised. By this means, as noted, the Lord's portion was recognizable in that, like sheep in a flock belonging to the emperor, each of them bore the circumcision as a kind of brand on his hidden member. And this was so arranged by God's wisdom in order that they not be confused with the other sheep, that is, with the gentiles, whose ignorance of God had reduced them to the level of wild beasts and unreasoning animals. So, why was it not prescribed that the brand be on some other part of the body rather than on this one? Because it is from this member that the seed comes forth and the fleshly birth of every man is effected. In addition, God sketches for us by this means a figure of the whole man stripped of the flesh, such that by this sign the Israelites might become both recognizable as children of the flesh, and provide a type of the spiritual circumcision of those children of the Spirit who would later be begotten without emission, or sexual intercourse, or corruption. Thus, when the latter circumcision appears, the former will at the same time cease, and each of the sheep in the circumcision of the flesh shall be branded instead with the blood of Christ, that is, with the circumcision not made by hands, as St Paul says, and with the putting-off of the flesh [cf. Col 2:11], by which I take it he means being earthly-minded. Being thus circumcised mystically, we yet become aware of it by the perception and knowledge of our soul.

V.

TWO OTHER WORLDS

Israel: an intermediary world and the promise of a better

This people, which was of the seed of Abraham and which comprised the portion taken from Adam's side, was established by God as a kind of new world, a third one, bearing in itself an image of that first creation and of Paradise, as well as of the second, that is, of the contents of the Ark. Nor this alone, but it was also a type of things which would happen afterwards, in the future. It was a kind of intermediary, at once signifying the past in the future and showing that future and past are joined. For it possessed the Promised Land as another, second Paradise in place of the original garden. It had the ark in place of the Theotokos, and by means of these types it both declared and represented for us in images the return and inheritance which, by the renewal of the Holy Spirit, would come to pass for the saints in the world to come. It had the Law as our ancestors [Adam and Eve] had the commandments, and through the servitude of the Law it made plain the future freedom beyond law which would be given in the spiritual law. It possessed the jar of manna in place of the tree of life which stood in the middle of the garden and of which Adam and Eve were not permitted to eat. This image pointed ahead toward the vessel which would carry Christ within. It had the manna in place of Christ, since the Latter is the Bread Who came down from Heaven to give the world everlasting life. Thus the manna was also from Heaven, as it says in Scripture: "Man ate of the bread of angels" [Ps 78:25]. In summary, God made this people a new paradise. He placed within it much that was more precious and noble than the original, to such a degree, indeed, that it was in turn the type of still greater promises and realities.

Here, too, God placed Moses as He had placed Adam there. God spoke with him as He had to Adam, and Moses spoke with God as Adam had done. Unlike Moses, however, Adam had no hope of a promise that there, in Eden, God the only-begotten Son would appear in a body. The first Paradise had the tree of life, but not that which is Life itself. The second, however, possessed the grace of the Spirit more plainly than the tree of life in the prophets who announced the true and perfect life to be given in Christ. The first Paradise possessed a life without effort or care, with trees and beautiful fruit for food. The second had ready-made for food the manna from heaven. They "drank from the rock which followed them" [I Cor 10:4] water which was sweeter than honey. Nor this alone, for "neither their clothes nor their shoes grew old nor wore out" [Dt 8:4; 29:5], but grew together with their bodies, and there was "no one among their tribes who grew weak" [Ps 104:37, LXX]. Those in the former Paradise were threatened with death and curses in the event they transgressed the commandments. Those in the latter had hope of forgiveness of sins and the blessing of life everlasting in case some of them did not fulfill the Law of God. It was promised that the Christ would come and make possible what was impossible for them, not to condemn those who could not keep the Law, but to save those who believed. The first had the fiery sword to guard the entry to the tree of life and keep Adam and his issue away. The second had the Archangel Michael who watched over and protected those within while not permitting the gentiles scattered abroad to enter. In the first Paradise God had arranged beforehand that the re-creation of Adam should come to pass through his rib. For this reason, then, the woman was created from the man without intercourse, in order that later the rib taken from Adam might be born through a woman without emission or intercourse, be born a man who is Christ and God, that through Him Adam might be renewed. In the latter Paradise, God promised beforehand to Abraham that in his seed He would gather all the gentiles in exile and so make of them a single flock.

Israel's failure leads to greater blessings

Now, when those who enjoyed these good things had, both before and after their entry into the promised land, transgressed God's commandment which said: "Hear, O Israel, the Lord your God is one Lord" [Dt 6:4], and "You shall not bow down to any strange god" [cf. Ex 20:3 and 5]; and when "They sacrificed their sons and daughters to the demons" [Ps 107:37], "and ate and drank the wine of their drink offerings" [Dt 32:38], and "bowed down to the work of their hands, to what their own fingers have made" [Is 2:8], and "both killed the saints and stoned the prophets" [Mt 23:37], and "turned away like a deceitful bow" [Ps 78:57], and "with foreign gods and their abominations provoked the God Who had nourished them in the wilderness, and forgot Him" [Dt 32:21 and 18]—what then did the Lord do Who had chosen them out of all the nations? Did He become furious and turn away from them? By no means! Instead, He sent His Son to wash away their sins, since they, too, had come to the point of resembling the nations, as it is written: "They mingled with the nations and learned to do as they did" [Ps 106:35], and "They did not understand what their dignity was" [Ps 48:21, LXX]. So then, remember with me the Ark, the sons of Noah, and the wild beasts and reptiles which at that time entered into it. As I have said in explaining the contents of the Ark, Noah is a type of Christ, his sons of the people under the Law, and the beasts and reptiles of the nations. Now, the people who are under the Law, who are called the Lord's portion, His lot, have become like the beasts, that is, like the gentiles. And, desiring to recall them and establish them again in their ancient estate, God came down to earth and, taking the side of Adam from the all-pure flesh of the Theotokos, took flesh and became man, was made like us in every respect except for sin [Heb 4:15]. Why this? So that He could both perfect those who had kept the Law through faith in Him, and, by means of faith, join those who had committed fornication with idolatry to the rest of the body, and so as well might the nations be saved in the same way, by faith, according to what was said by St Paul: "For if their transgression means riches for the world...how much more will their salvation mean?" [Rom 11:12]

The contemplation of this saying, however, so far as its letter goes, clearly suggests to me another consideration. So, pay attention and learn what the divine Apostle means when he says: "If their trespass means riches for the world...how much more must their salvation mean?"

VI.

A DRAMATIZATION OF THE NATIONS AND OF ISRAEL

Out of the scattering of the nations, as I said above, Israel became the Lord's portion. Now this Israel, having become a great nation and a populous people, then fell into an idolatry just like that of the gentiles. A very few, like a kind of leaven, were preserved as a portion for God. If they had believed in Christ when He did come, and had worshipped Him as God, then all of them, just and unjust, God-fearing and idolatrous, would have become one, and at the same time would have been saved. And, if this had happened, then the gentiles would have spoken up and said to Him: "God and Master of all, Lord of the ages, behold all these whom You have saved without respect to any works of righteousness. What, then? Are not we, too, the works of Your hands and of Your fashioning?"

The Jews would have answered them with what in fact they did say: "No, but we ourselves alone are His portion; we alone His lot. The tablets of the covenant, the circumcision, and the rest—these are ours, promised to us alone, and given just to us. To you, though, He will never give anything."

In reply, the gentiles would again raise an objection, though without reckoning the envious Jews worthy of an answer:

O Master and Word of God, You rightly rejected us as unworthy, abandoning us who were heedless as stiff-necked and disobedient, and You justly left us to a famine of ignorance and a waterless thirst so as not to hear Your holy words. But, You showed every love and concern for these people here. You gave them judges and prophets and teachers as guides and tutors. You made the Law for them, and circumcision, and signs and wonders. And they reckoned all these things as nothing. They abandoned You and bowed down with us to idols as if to gods, and whatever works we did—all of them—they did as well. But now, when by virtue of their faith alone You have been compassionate with them, have pitied and had mercy on them, and have numbered them with Your saints who did no sin, will You not have mercy on us, too? Will You not have mercy on us? Will You not, O Lover of mankind, accept even us?

And so, with justice and reason, those of the uncircumcision would have been joined with the circumcised who had sacrificed to idols, and all would have become one in Christ.

But, since the Jews, on top of all their former evils, both slew Him Who was Christ and God as a criminal, asking instead for Barabbas as an antitype of the Antichrist and then freeing him, and afterwards persecuted His Apostles, God, as we have said, exiled them from Paradise and scattered them among the gentiles, because they had taken up the nations' impiety instead [of Him]. As for the nations who had issued from the side of Adam, He Who had taken Adam's rib from the woman and had fashioned it into a perfect man, Who had become flesh and taken the title of a son of Adam according to Adam's own nature, Who was Himself wholly by nature Son and Word of God, the Same drew them to Himself.

Here is all the wealth of the world! And, if such became the world's wealth, how much the more so would the Jews have become part of it had they believed! From the time of first dispersion [i.e., following Babel and the election of Abraham] the chosen portion was the whole of Israel, whom God had foreknown and predestined. And, when He came, He called Israel to believe in Him. But, because Israel did not want to come to Him, He took from the whole portion as a small part those who did believe in Him, which is to say, John the Forerunner, the Apostles, and those who followed them. The greater part of the portion, which had fallen into unbelief by its own free choice, He cast away. The gentiles entered instead of them and, by faith, were joined in their turn to the portion of election by faith.

Now, at this point, look with me at how our discourse has progressed on its way, at how what is proper to the new and wonderful portion comes to be set forth.

VII.

THE CHURCH OF CHRIST IS A NEW WORLD, AND FAITH IN HIM A NEW PARADISE

Not a type, but the truth

Once again, we have the beginning of a new portion and a new world, and with that portion a mixture which is strange, new, and paradoxical. Up to this point, all were types and shadows, riddles of this. But this, this *is* the truth. This is both the renovation and the renewal of the whole world. For the portion taken from Adam became corrupt and, growing into a great multitude of corrupt and mortal people, was destroyed entirely by the flood. Of it, Noah alone survived and, together with his sons, comprised a portion distilled from the first, the beginning of a second world. When men once again sought to climb up into heaven, God, Who had promised never again to make a flood nor destroy all the flesh living on the earth, took once more as His portion Abraham, according to the election of faith, and scattered all others throughout the world. Then, from this portion of Abraham, the very God Himself assumed a portion of his seed—the side of Adam of which I have spoken so often—and built a habitation for Himself. He built it of flesh and without change He became man—but not merely a man! For He did not become the first-fruits of fleshly children, of a corruptible people such as Noah had become before, a people that, in perishing even as it multiplied, would become in its turn the first-fruits of yet another people's subsequent genesis. No, He became rather the immortal and ever-living first-fruits of spiritual children, children who are ever being formed anew according to His imprint. As the Apostle says: "Christ the first-fruits, then...those who belong to Christ" [I Cor 15:23]; and elsewhere: "...until Christ be formed in us" [Gal 4:19]. While all those who are our ancestors were mortal, He Who took up the portion from the seed of Abraham, He Who is Son of God, is incorrupt and immortal, and He does not beget children in a fleshly way, but He re-fashions us instead spiritually.

The new paradise

Now, consider with me the manner of this re-fashioning. What is it? In Paradise, the woman was born from the man, and she was mother of all who are born from the earth. In the Church of the faithful, however, Christ our God was born a man of the woman, the first-fruits and life of all who out of their faith in Him are spiritually re-born. There [in Paradise], there was a tree of knowledge of good and evil which became the cause of death for those who partook of it. Here, there is the tree of the Cross to which Christ, the second Adam and God, was nailed. He was nailed by His hands, in place of Adam's hands which had handled the fruit [of the first tree], and by His feet, in place of the feet which had walked toward the [first] transgression. While Adam, in feasting from that tree became the origin of death and a curse for all who were born of him, He Who is Christ and God, in tasting bitter gall and drinking vinegar, released Adam's descendants from the curse and freed them from the corruption of death. He granted new life to those who believe in Him, and enabled them to lead in this world a way of life which is new and equal to the angels. There, the tree of life stood in the middle of Paradise and, by God's economy, Adam was not permitted to eat of it, but was instead cast out of the garden while the flaming sword was set to guard its entry. Here, Christ was pierced in His side with the spear, and turned aside that sword, and opened the entry-way, and planted the tree of life in the midst of the whole world. Indeed, He has given us authority each day to plant this tree which grows up in an instant and provides life everlasting to all who eat of it.

O Paradise planted anew by Christ our God! O new mystery and dreadful wonders! There, Adam and Eve lived avowedly among trees which were physical and visible. Both the tree of knowledge and the tree of life were different from each other. But here, the new Adam becomes all things at once for those who believe, both food and a knowledge which does not lead to death nor banish us from the tree of life, but rather which teaches us with what words the serpent ought instead to have been answered: "Get behind me, Satan!" He said [Mt 4:10ff], together with the rest. Nor is this all, but that knowledge leads us to the Life which, again, is He Himself. "But," you say, "where is this new paradise which you say Christ has made? Look and see! The whole world is just the same as it was when it was made. And we live on the earth in which we were condemned to eat our bread by effort and toil and by the sweat of our brow. Where is this Paradise that you are telling us about?" If you do want to learn about the works and mysteries of the invisible and incomprehensible God, mysteries which are invisible and incomprehensible for those who do not believe, then open up your mind to what we have to say and you will indeed learn and understand them.

The sequence of the Fall is reversed in God's economy

First of all, God made heaven and earth and everything which is in them, and, after all this, He formed man with His own hands. Then He made Paradise and all that it contained, and placed within it the man whom He had made. Then, after He had taken one of the man's ribs and built it up into a woman, He commanded them both not to eat from the tree of the knowledge of good and evil, so that they should not die in death but instead work in accordance with the commandment and keep it. They, however, first turned away from the remembrance of God and of His good works—which remembrance was itself the work which God had given them—and, secondly, they abandoned their keeping of the commandment and ate of the tree which He had ordered them not to eat of. Thus immediately they suffered the death of their souls and then later, after many years, bodily death, and so they were brought down to Hell. They were not alone to suffer this. So, too, suffered all who were born of them up to the coming of Christ God, the new Adam, and His descent into Hell and resurrection from the dead. When, however, He came Who had created all things before and Who now wished to renew them, He did not wish to renew them according to the same sequence by which He had created them before. How, then? First He would renew the man, and then afterwards the creation. In what way, and why? Because, while He had then first prepared all the visible creation for Adam's habitation and enjoyment, as his kingdom, and then directly afterwards created the man, now, on the other hand, if He had wanted first of all to renew creation and render it spiritual and incorruptible and eternal, where in that case would the man have been able to dwell, clothed as he was in corruptible flesh, an animal and mortal? In what world would he then have been able to live, to marry and be married, to beget and be born, and to grow up in? You have no answer, truly. So, for this reason God first raised up the man who had fallen, been broken, and grown old, re-created and renewed him, and then subsequently the creation.

Now, though, just as we have spoken in sequence about the creation and its fall, so we must speak as well about its renewal. Consider the parallelism of the things of old, with what balance they parallel the economy and covenant of God. Thus, first, Adam was introduced into Paradise and then Eve was brought forth. Even so, first the Son of God, Himself the Creator of Adam, came down and entered into the pure womb of the Virgin, and then received from her the rib of Adam, which is to say, her all-pure flesh, and became man, and, in place of Eve who had been deceived by the serpent, He went forth into the world as the new Adam come to slay the serpent, Eve's seducer. First Eve was deceived, after the serpent had spoken to her, then ate of the tree and transgressed the commandment, and so died the death of the soul. First is Mary, the Theotokos, given the good news by the angel, and believes in God's will as announced to her, and consents to it, saying: "Behold the handmaid of the Lord; let it be to me according to your word" [Lk 1:38]. So was she the first to receive in herself substantially the Word of God, and to have her soul thus redeemed from that eternal death. And, the moment the Word was made flesh, He re-created the body of Adam, immediately breathing into it His breath to make of it a living soul. For, when He had originally taken the rib, it was already ensouled, and He then built it up into the woman—since it is not written that the breath was also created. Now, in order to make our point more clearly, let us look again at this passage.

Adam's side a type of the Church and of the Eucharist

God took from Adam that portion of his flesh and filled up its space with [new] flesh, and then built up what He had taken into a complete human being. As for a soul, He added nothing to Adam in place of what He had taken with the rib itself, nor indeed did He increase it in Eve. Rather, while as it were the flesh received in place of the rib was added, the soul was not yet supplemented. But, again, listen to this which is more clear. God took from the

Virgin flesh endowed with a mind and soul, the [same] flesh which He had taken from Adam, and replaced it with other flesh in its stead. Having taken this same from her, He gave it His own Spirit, the Holy Spirit, and enlarged it with what its soul had not had before: life everlasting. The flesh which had taken the place of the rib in Adam's body was the earnest and surety of God's economy. It is as if He were to take from the rib another rib, and give in its stead—not flesh, for that had already been supplied—but the Spirit which is essentially of God, so that, just as the woman came to be from Adam's side and all mortal men from her, so the man Christ, Who is God, comes into being from the flesh of the woman, and from Him in turn all men are named immortal, and Adam thus receives a supplement greater than what he had earlier received in place of the woman. What is it then that he received which was more? The flesh in his body which replaced his rib. For, to repeat myself, when Christ took flesh of the Virgin, He was obliged once more to replace it, just as He replaced what Adam had lost. Because, once again, the replacement [in the Theotokos] was not oriented toward corruption, but occurred for the sake of incorruption, it took the form of Spirit, and not of flesh, in order for Him to re-create the nature of Adam, and so that the children who would be born of God might receive regeneration through the Holy Spirit, and thus that all who believe in Him might become, in the Spirit, God's own kin and so comprise [with Him] one single body.

And, in the same way that it was said of the original couple: "On account of this"—On account of what? Clearly, of the woman, I mean, of Adam's side—"a man leaves his father and his mother and cleaves to his wife"—that is, to Adam's side—"and the two become one flesh" [Gen 2:24]. The same applies to Christ our God. For, because He took flesh from the all-pure blood of the Theotokos (and bestowed on her in return the Holy Spirit), He was both made flesh and became man. Thus, on account of this (or Him), a man will leave his father and his mother—and in addition

his wife and children and brothers and sisters—and cleave—not
to the woman nor to the flesh but, as all of us are from the woman
who are born in the body—to the man Who was born without seed
of the woman, to Christ the Bridegroom. And thus, spiritually
joined and cleaving to Him, we shall each one be with Him one
Spirit and likewise one body, by virtue of our bodily eating His
flesh and drinking His blood.

This is no more than what our Lord and God Himself declared:
"He who eats My flesh and drinks My blood abides in Me and I
in him" [Jn 6:56]. With this godly saying the word thus spoken by
the Apostle agrees: "He who joins himself to a prostitute becomes
one body with her...But he who is united to the Lord becomes one
Spirit with Him" [I Cor 6:16-17]. We become one, I say, not in
our persons, but one in the nature of divinity and of humanity. We
are one in the nature of divinity on becoming ourselves gods by
adoption, according to what was said by John the Evangelist:
"And we know that when He appears, we shall be like Him" [I Jn
3:2]. How so? Because "From His fulness have we all received"
[Jn 1:16]. On the other hand, we are one in the nature of humanity
as His kinfolk, and as having been accorded the name of His
brothers, just as we have said elsewhere. Our holy fathers knew
this when they said plainly: "Give blood and receive the Spirit,"[4]
inasmuch as the Spirit is not otherwise given us than through our
voluntary crucifixion and dying to the world. For God, Who is
Spirit according to the Scripture [Jn 4:24], wills that by the Holy
Spirit we be united to Him and cleave to Him, become one body
and co-heirs with Him, as the whole divine Scripture bears witness. But, let us return to the matter before us.

Now then, God the Word took flesh from the pure Theotokos
and gave in its place not flesh, but the Spirit Who is by essence
Holy. And through the Latter He vivified first of all her precious
and most spotless soul, and raised her up from death. He did this

4 Longinus 5, *Apophthegmata*, PG 65.257B.

because it was Eve who was first to die the death of the soul. He was made flesh and became man, possessing a body endowed with mind and soul. For this was the flesh imbued with soul which before He had ineffably taken from Adam and now takes from the Theotokos, and thus He mysteriously renews our entire nature. Born in manner inexpressible, as He alone knows, He entered into the world. For what cause, and why? In order to seek out Adam, who had been exiled in this world, and, finding him, to create him anew. And now, repeating here what I have said above, do consider with me the fearful mystery of God's economy.

Repentance and predestination to salvation

While he was still in Paradise, Adam was called to repentance. For God said to him: "Adam, where are you?"; and: "Who told you that you were naked? Have you eaten of the tree of which I told you not to eat?" [Gen 3:9 and 11]. Yet, when he heard this, he did not want to repent, or to weep, or beseech forgiveness. But why? He makes the woman responsible for his foolishness and his sin. Therefore he is indeed rightly thrown out of Paradise. Because Adam did not want at the time to repent, and because this was at the counsel of the evil demon, for the same reason God, when He comes on the earth, calls everyone to Himself through repentance, saying: "Repent, for the Kingdom of Heaven is at hand" [Mt 4:17]. He is at hand. He stands at the gates of your hearts and minds. Open your hearts through faith and He will enter immediately, and, at the same moment, your mouths will be opened up, and you will cry: "We have the treasure of the Spirit within us" [cf. II Cor 4:7]. We have it! We possess in our hearts life everlasting! Consider this: God called the Jews first of all, and they were not persuaded to depart from their ways. Lastly, He calls all the nations through His Son and, persuaded, they run and flee to Him. Therefore, He also says to His Apostles: "Go out quickly to the streets and lanes, and bring in the poor and maimed and blind and lame" [Lk 14:21]. By "city" He means all this world. "Streets and alleys" mean the tribes of the nations, and the countries which are hidden and far away. "Poor and maimed, both blind and lame" means those who are tormented by their many sins and different faults and lawlessness, and by their ignorance of God.

He invites everyone from east to west, I mean both Hebrews and Greeks. As we have often said, He, as God, knew beforehand the disobedience of the Hebrews by reason of their faithlessness, and the conversion of the gentiles out of faith. And, before the ages, He predestined that as many as should believe in Him and be baptized in His name, that is, in the name of the Father and of the Son and of the Holy Spirit, and eat the pure body of His Son and drink His precious blood, would be justified from sin, which is to say, would be freed and glorified, and become partakers of life everlasting—just as He Himself, the Master of all, has said: "He who eats My flesh and drinks My blood has everlasting life" [Jn 6:54], and: "He does not come into judgement, but has passed from death to life" [Jn 5:24]. So then, my brother, see how you were foreknown by God, and predestined, and glorified, and justified, and called up into everlasting life through faith in Christ and holy Baptism. And you were not, as Adam before, introduced to a physical paradise, but to Heaven and the good things which are in Heaven, which "No eye has seen, nor ear heard, nor the heart of man conceived" [I Cor 2:9]. Therefore, work at the virtues and keep God's commandments. Rather, by means of the commandments keep yourself from transgressing anything which has been ordered of you, lest indeed you yield to Adam's example—or even to worse—and be deprived of the greater and heavenly good things. Do not prefer anything terrestrial, nor let any lust overpower you, so that you not be stripped of the glory with which you have been glorified by Christ and, as not robed in a wedding garment, be bound hand and foot, and be cast into the outer darkness where there is wailing and gnashing of teeth. [Mt 22:11-13]

Faith in Christ is the new Paradise. Thus God knew before the foundation of the world all who believed and will believe in Him, whom He called and will not cease calling until the end, whom He glorified and will glorify, justified and will justify; those, clearly, whom He reveals as conformed to the glory of the image of His Son through holy Baptism and the grace of the Holy Spirit. He makes them mystically all His sons, and establishes them as new out of old, immortals out of mortals, and gives them commandments as once He gave to Adam. As many, then, as shall keep His commandments until death, the same show forth their love for God and ascend progressively toward yet greater glory. As many, however, as are contemptuous and inattentive and ungrateful regarding their Benefactor, and will not keep the commandments which were given by Him, will fall from these good things like Adam fell from Paradise—not because they were not foreknown by God, but as suffering from their own foolishness and evil. On this account, therefore, God also placed within this Paradise the saving medicine of repentance, such that those who fall from everlasting life out of sloth and inattention may ascend to it again with a brighter and more resplendent glory. For, unless the God Who loves mankind had arranged for this, no flesh would be saved. [Mt 24:22]

So, putting aside every other concern, let us attend so far as we are able to repentance, so that we may attain to the present and future good things, by the grace and love for mankind of our Lord Jesus Christ, to Whom be glory and majesty unto ages of ages. Amen.

THIRD ETHICAL DISCOURSE

Introduction

Discourse III provides, as we noted above, something of a transition from the cosmic redemption sketched in the first two treatises to the ways in which salvation is appropriated by the individual believer in *Discourses* IV-XI. It is based on the experience of "rapture" in the "third heaven" and the hearing of "ineffable speech" which St Paul, the model mystic for Symeon, reports in II Corinthians 12:2-4. What, asks the New Theologian, was the "ineffable speech" which the Apostle heard and, secondly, how may we experience now what he experienced then? In reply to the first, Symeon develops an analogy between the human soul and the Holy Trinity in order to arrive at the conclusion that the Apostle enjoyed a single perception of the divine glory, a perception wherein vision is the most important element but where all the other senses are fulfilled as well. St Paul saw—and heard and tasted and smelled and felt—the one light which is God. As to how we may know this ourselves, Symeon first reiterates his insistence in the second discourse that we have only to desire and will it, i.e., believe and obey the commandments, and, secondly, he affirms that the good things seen by St Paul are the same Body and Blood of Christ made available to the Christian in the Eucharist and perceived by grace in the Holy Spirit. To deny this, he insists, is to place oneself in the same category as the Jews in John 6 who will not accept Christ's teaching on the Eucharist because they cannot—or better, will not—see Who He truly is, but instead perceive Him as merely a man. The glory of God is present now in the Church's sacraments, and to see that glory we must ask for and receive the same Holy Spirit Who effects the change of bread and wine into Christ's body and blood.

THE INEFFABLE WORDS WHICH PAUL HEARD

On the obvious and the hidden in Christ's teaching

Since, truly, the Master of all clearly cries out to us every day in the Gospels, now saying it in obscure manner when He speaks in parables, now explaining in private to His own disciples as follows: "To you it has been given to know the secrets of the Kingdom of God, but for others they are in parables" [Lk 8:10], and at other times speaking to us boldly and without veils, such that the disciples reply: "Ah! now you are speaking plainly, and not in figures" [Jn 16:29], we are thus obliged to search out and learn what it is that our Lord says boldly and nakedly, and what it is that He says in parables. The meaning of the commandments is plain and unclothed, as when the Gospel says: "Love your enemies," do good to those who hate you [Mt 5:44], or: "Repent, for the Kingdom of Heaven is at hand" [Mt 4:17], and again: "Whoever wishes to save his life shall lose it, whoever loses his life for My sake shall find it to life everlasting" [Mt 10:39], and: "If anyone would come after Me, let him deny himself and take up his cross, and follow Me" [Mt 16:24]. These sayings, together with those which follow them, are not in parables but, to the contrary, are spoken plainly without any hidden meaning. Others, however, are in parables, as when He says:

> To what shall I liken the Kingdom of God? It is like a grain of mustard seed which a man took and sowed in his field, and when it had grown, it became a great tree... [Mt 13:31ff];

or when He says: "The Kingdom of Heaven is like a man in search of fine pearls" [Mt 13:45]; and again: "The Kingdom of Heaven is like leaven which a woman took and hid in three measures of flour, until it was all leavened" [Mt 13:33]. When He says such things, and still others, and compares the Kingdom of Heaven to them, this He calls speaking in parables.

Now consider God's wisdom with me here, how, by using examples of things which appear to us to be of little significance, He outlines what surpasses our intellect and reason. And He does all this in order that those who are unbelieving, and by consequence of their unbelief become unworthy of such matters, may remain blind and have no portion in these good things, and that the believers, who receive the word of the parables with assurance, may behold the manifest fulfillment of what occurs in them, the truth itself. For these parables are images of things which are actually happening. Listen to how this is so. The grain of mustard is the Holy Spirit, and the latter—understand me well!—is nothing other than the Kingdom of Heaven. The man is every believer who wants to receive this seed by doing the commandments. The field is no other place than the heart of each one of us. It is there [in our hearts] that we receive and hide that one seed which is not many, nor divisible, but Who is by nature undivided and inseparable. While we keep and watch over ourselves with all vigilance, it grows in a manner we do not know, and we behold it established in ourselves. When it has grown, it is known the more by those in whom it was planted, and, when it has become a tree and put out many branches, it produces an inexpressible joy in those who possess it. Just as the field without seed produces nothing useful except for thorns and weeds, and just as the seed bears no fruit without being planted in the field, but remains alone just as it was, so, truly, do our own souls remain fruitless without the divine seed and yield nothing save thorns. Before being sown in us, I mean in our hearts, the divine seed remains itself, wholly God, neither accepting addition nor suffering subtraction, and so within us is neither planted nor admits any growth. For how could someone apart from that seed reveal its power of growth in the same way as those who have in fact united themselves with it? In no way! So fire will never ignite any matter with which it has not come into contact, nor will matter burst into flame unless it has been substantially joined to fire.

The "ineffable speech" heard by St Paul

Now, just as with the sayings of the Gospels, where some are
given to us obscurely and, as was noted, through parables, and
some are spoken boldly and without any veils, just so is it with
respect to the God-inspired words of the Apostles. Not everything
is given to us plainly and unveiled. Rather, on occasion, these also
require a great deal of examination and interpretation due to the
profundity of thought and mystery which they somehow bear.
And now, if you please, we shall see what are the depths of the
Spirit since, as Scripture says: "The Spirit searches everything,
even the depths of God" [I Cor 2:10].

What then is our subject, the point of departure for this
discourse? It is the "ineffable speech" which the divine Paul heard
when he was taken up in rapture to the third heaven. But, let us
start at the beginning and ask first of all what the meaning of
"speech" is, in order that we may proceed thus step by step in
appreciating the real power of the Apostle's words. "Speech
[*rhêma*]" means "word [*logos*]", just as "word" is also called
"speech." For, as Scripture says, "Say the word [*logos*], and my
servant will be healed" [Mt 8:8]; and in Job: "Say a word [*rhêma*]
against God, and die" [Job 2:9]; and elsewhere: "The speech
[*rhêmata*] of His mouth" [Ps 36:3]. Men's speech and words are
both spoken by their mouths and heard by their ears, but God's
speech and word, coming forth from His mouth, are entirely
unutterable for human tongues and wholly inaccessible to fleshly
hearing. Indeed, they are entirely inaccessible to human perception, since our perception is clearly unable to perceive that which
transcends perception.

Christ is the Father's "speech" and His "mouth" the
Holy Spirit

Thus, according to our first attempt at interpretation, we know
that "speech" and "word" mean nothing other than the Son of God

the Father, our Lord Jesus Christ Himself, Who is true God, and that the Father's mouth which utters the "ineffable speech" is none other than His Holy and consubstantial Spirit, just as the prophet will say "For the mouth of the Lord has spoken" [Is 1:20] instead of the Holy Spirit. God's "mouth" is therefore the Holy Spirit while His "speech" and "word" is God the Son. Why is the Spirit called God's mouth and the Son His speech and word? Because, just as the word which is in us goes out through our mouths and is revealed to others, and is otherwise impossible to say or to make clear except by the utterance of the mouth, so can God's Son and Word not be made known or heard unless He be spoken—that is, revealed—by the Holy Spirit as by a mouth.[1] We say "cannot" here, rather than "will not" or "does not wish," in the same sense that we say God cannot be false [Heb 6:18]. Just as our word, closed up within us, cannot come out unless we open our mouths, just so unless God's mouth, which is to say His Holy Spirit, opens up by virtue of the illumination which comes to pass in us—though it is not the Spirit Who opens up, but our mind which is illumined by Him—the Son and Word of God is neither seen, nor made known, nor indeed revealed at all to our senses of sight and hearing.

Thus the "ineffable speech" which the divine Paul heard is nothing other, by our modest reasoning, than the mystical and truly inexpressible contemplations, the transcendently splendid and unknowable knowledge given by the illumination of the Holy Spirit, by which we mean the invisible visions of the glory and divinity, beyond light and transcending knowledge, of the Son and Word of God. These contemplations, revealed the more manifestly and clearly to those who are worthy of them, show themselves as the inaudible auditions of unutterable speech, the comprehension through incomprehension of things incomprehensible. And, if the Apostle says: "I heard ineffable speech," we for our

1 For this image of "word" and "breath" cf. Gregory of Nyssa, *The Great Catechism* 2 (Srawley, 13-15).

part say that this is the Son of God the Father, declared by the Holy
Spirit and, by the Latter's illumination, revealed to those who are
worthy. Now, if the illumination or revelation occurs as a vision,
rather than by hearing, do not be put off by this but, instead, listen
to our solution of this matter and learn to be believing and not
incredulous. Our reply is as follows.

The soul in the likeness of the Trinity: a single perception[2]

God, the cause of all, is One. This One is light and life, spirit
and word, mouth and speech, wisdom and knowledge, joy and
love, the Kingdom of Heaven and Paradise, the heaven of heavens, just as He is called the sun of suns, God of gods, day without
evening, and whatever other good thing you might cite from the
visible world. And, if you seek beyond all that exists, you will find
this One Who is, and is alone properly and substantially called
Good. That One is not such as are visible things. Rather, He
transcends incomparably and inalterably all the visible world.
Neither will you find that that One exists in the same manner as
visible things, separate and distinct. He abides instead without
alteration and is the Same, at once all-good and transcending all
that is good. It is thus that man, created according to the image and
likeness of God, is also honored. He possesses a single perception
in a unique soul and intellect and reason. While this perception is
divided up five ways according to the physical necessities of the
body, it manifests its activity by changing unchangeably, such that
it is not sight which sees, but the soul which sees by means of
sight, and the same holds true for hearing and smelling, for tasting,
and for distinguishing by touch. With regard to spiritual matters,
however, the soul is no longer obliged to discern through the
windows of the senses. It no longer seeks to open the eyes in order

2 In developing the image sketched above, Symeon launches here
  into a complete parallel between the human soul and the Trinity.
  On this feature of his thought, see our *Introduction*, Part II,
  forthcoming in volume III.

to see or contemplate some existing thing, nor the ears in order to admit discourse. Neither does it require lips or tongue in order to distinguish sweet from bitter, nor hands in order to know by means of them what is rough, or soft, or smooth. Rather, perception goes outside all of these and is gathered together wholly within the intellect, as being naturally consequent upon the latter and inseparably one with it. To put it more precisely, it possesses the five senses within itself as one rather than several.

Now, consider with me an exact examination of the question. Soul, intellect, and reason, as we said, are one. They exist in a single being and nature. It is this one thing which perceives, reasons—for it is rational—thinks, plans, remembers, deliberates, desires, wills, or does not will, chooses, or does not choose, loves, and hates. Not to go on at length, this one being is a living thing, at once seeing and hearing, smelling, tasting and touching, knowing, recognizing, making known, and thus speaking. Pay close attention to the sense of what I am saying, so that you may become able thus to learn what that "ineffable speech" is, together with how Paul heard those things which were revealed to him and which, in the divine Spirit, he also beheld. God is One, the Creator of all. This One is therefore every thing which is good, as we said. The rational and immortal soul is one. This one soul is every perception, that is, it possesses the senses, as many as there are, within itself. Therefore, when the one God of all appears in revelation to the one and rational soul, every good thing is revealed to it and appears to it at one and the same time through all of its senses. He [God] is both seen and heard, is sweet to the taste and perfume to the sense of smell; He is felt and so made known. He both speaks and is spoken. He knows, and is recognized, and is perceived as knowing. For the one who is known by God knows that he is known, and he who sees God knows that God sees him. He who does not see God, however, does not know that God sees him, in that he does not see, though he may see everything else and miss nothing.

The equivalence in Scripture of "seeing" and "hearing"

So it is that those who have been deemed worthy see by means of all of their senses Him Who is all-good and yet transcends every good thing. As by a single perception compounded of many senses they grasp Him Who is Himself both One and Many. They have recognized, and daily recognize, through the different facets of that one perception, that these many and varied good things are at once as one. They understand no distinction in these things, but call contemplation knowledge and knowledge again contemplation. They call vision hearing, and hearing vision. It is as when Habbakuk says: "Lord, I have heard the hearing [*akoê*] of You and I was afraid. Lord, I have learned of Your works and I was amazed" [Hab 3:2, LXX]. From whom else did he hear? Prophesying of God, he proclaimed Him. And how does he say: "I have heard of the hearing of You"? What does he mean to clarify by the duplication of "hearing," unless it be that, by the illumination or revelation of the Spirit, he has learned of our Lord, the Son of God, and has in turn by the Latter's prompting been apprised of the Economy of salvation and, as it were, has made his own that teaching concerning Him which he has learned from Him? It is as seeing the Lord and being seen by Him that he says to Him with joy: "In the midst of the animals You will be known; in the approaching years You will be recognized; in the passage of time You will shine forth" [Hab 3:2, LXX]. So he calls "hearing" the teaching and knowledge which have come to him in his contemplation of the Spirit's glory, which he heard concerning the Lord's becoming man and His appearance on the earth. And this itself, that is, to say "Lord," has the sense of both seeing and speaking to Him. For who addresses someone as if he did see him when he does not? Could someone who does not see the earthly emperor say to him: "O Emperor, I have heard what your Majesty has declared"? Of course not! Does the prophet say that he merely "heard" about Him, but not rather that He will be made known, will be recognized and reveal Himself, demonstrating that he has learned with complete assurance of His will and so, as it were, saying to Him: "You shall do this and that, Master, as has been decreed by Your Majesty"? And still greater things than this are suggested by all the prophets' sayings.

The holy Scripture thus habitually uses the vision of God to mean hearing and hearing to mean vision. Thus, too, the divine Paul called his unutterable visions and illuminations "speech," those teachings and revelations which exceed the measure of human nature and ability, and said that he had "heard" these things and put them into writing. So, too, he said: "And to keep me from being too elated by the abundance of revelations, a thorn was given me in the flesh" [II Cor 12:7]. Now, if first of all he "heard," how after this does he call "revelations" [lit., "unveilings"] the things he heard if it was not as we said it was? For David, too, prays in this way, that his eyes may be opened to know the wonders of God from His Law [Ps 119:18]. When Paul says earlier, "Whether in the body or out of the body, I do not know; I was caught up," how then does he say "I heard" unless it happened as we have made clear in detail above, and that this is the truth of the matter? Therefore it is obvious that he indicated the vision first with the expression "taken up," while that which was within the vision and which was more expressly revelatory than the piercingly shining rays of glory and divinity, that is, which instilled knowledge and taught the seer, and made plain to him what is in every respect inexpressible and incomprehensible, he said he "heard." Clearly, he shows that the perceptions of hearing and of contemplation are one with respect to spiritual things. Thus it is that not one of the things heard or seen, as he saw and heard them, is he able ever to describe as what or what sort of thing it is, and therefore he adds that it is impossible for the human tongue to utter them.

The unity of mystical knowledge

So, let us strive to purify ourselves through repentance and humility, and to unite all our senses as one to the God Who is good, and transcends the good. Then, truly, everything which we have not quite been able to say or to demonstrate with our many words, you will be taught in an instant, all at once. You will hear with your sight, and see with your hearing. You will be taught while seeing and, again, hear what is unveiled. In addition, there is a certain other kind of hearing in the higher things of the Spirit. Of what kind is this? It is the promise of the good things which are to be given in the future. For, just as the Lord's first appearance was announced by the prophets, and although He was precisely made known to and seen by them, yet, because His coming had not yet taken place in their days but would happen afterwards, they said they heard what had been in fact unveiled and shown to them because this would only be accomplished in actuality in the future. In the same way Paul, too, who had seen the good things stored up for the righteous who struggle now, and who both knew and had learned precisely that those who have loved God with all their soul will receive these things following the Lord's second coming and the resurrection of the dead, put these matters in the form, as it were, of a declaration and a promise when he cried out: "I heard unutterable speech which it is not lawful for a man to speak." And what did he mean by calling these things "speech"? He said in effect "good things" and then "speech" because these good things are in truth a strange kind of speech, are words, by virtue of which every nature endowed with reason rejoices in genuinely inexhaustible and ever-living delight, and is divinely quickened, and is made to be glad. For, if the Word of God the Father is God, the illuminations of God the Word will justly be called "speech," since the word poured out at length in recitation is no longer a word, but is called a speech, as in: "Give ear to my speech, O Lord, give heed to the sound of my groaning. Hearken to the sound of my cry" [Ps 5:1-2].

God is therefore Word, and His speech the rays and illuminations of His divinity which, in the manner of a bolt of lightning, leap out and are borne—rather, revealed—to us who are quite incapable of articulating them. John, the disciple whom Christ

loved, spoke to the issue and, according to the grace which had
been given him, clarified a little what Paul had heard, saying:

> Brothers, we are God's children now; it is not yet evident
> what we shall be, but we know that when He appears, we
> shall be like Him. [I Jn 3:2]

The one said, "I heard unutterable speech which it is not lawful
for a man to speak," and the other, "We know that when He
appears we shall be like Him," and shall see Him more perfectly. Paul himself says the same: "Now I know in part; then
I shall know even as I am known" [I Cor 13:12]. There! You
see how, for those who are spiritual, knowledge and likeness,
contemplation and recognition, are one and the same. Thus
Christ becomes all things for us: knowledge, wisdom, word,
light, illumination, likeness, contemplation, recognition. Even
in the present life He gives to those who love Him that enjoyment, in part, of His own good things. He mysteriously allows
them both to sense with the intellect and to hear the ineffable
speech which is hidden for the many.

Christ is the master and the vesture of the wedding feast

If Christ were not all things at once for us, then the Kingdom
of Heaven and our delight in it would be lacking something.
Unless, in addition to what we have said, He were to become for
all who are righteous and who love Him vesture and crown and
sandal, joy and sweetness, food, drink, table, bed, rest, repose, the
irresistible beauty of contemplation, and everything else necessary for delight or for glory and pleasure, and if only one thing
were ever to be lacking for any one of those who sojourn in those
courts, then the privation of any good thing would immediately
allow for sorrow, and the latter would intrude on the unutterable
joy of those who rejoice. Thus the word of Scripture would prove
to be a lie which says: "Sorrow and sighing and pain shall flee
away" [Is 35:10]. But this shall not be, it shall not! Rather, He will
be all things for all, and every good thing in all good things, ever

super-abounding and filling up beyond measure all the perceptions of those who recline at the wedding feasts of Christ the King,
the Latter Himself being the One Who is uniquely eaten and
drunk, and every kind of food and drink and sweetness. At that
time, when seen by all and Himself seeing all those innumerable
multitudes, His own eye fixed forever and unchangingly in its
gaze, each of them will believe himself to be seen by Him, and no
one of them will sorrow as having been overlooked. The Same
shall be, as we have said, a crown set unalterably and unchangingly upon the heads of all the saints, one which reveals itself as
different for each of them, and He will distribute Himself among
them according to the dignity of each as each is worthy. He shall
Himself be the vesture of all, to the degree that each is eager at
that time to be clothed with Him, since no one enters the mystical
marriage without putting on that unapproachable gown. And if
someone were to slip himself in with the others and enter se-
cretly—which is impossible—he would as soon be thrown out.

Wishing to show us that no one enters there clothed in mourning, the Master made this clear in the parable when He said:
"Friend, how did you get in here without a wedding garment?"
and then: "Bind him hand and foot, and cast him into the outer
darkness" [Mt 22:12-13]. Now, I think that this was said not as if
the man had first sneaked past by Him Who is without error, but
because it was not yet time to reveal such mysteries. Because, at
that time, He did not want to say more plainly that "No one will
enter there without wearing the robe of My divinity," He uses this
saying to suggest it. Paul, too, when he had been taught this by
Christ speaking within him, said: "Just as we have borne the
image of the man of dust, we shall also bear the image of the man
of heaven" [I Cor 15:49]. Why? Because, he says: "As was the
man of dust, so are those who are of the dust; and as is the man of
heaven, so are those who are of heaven" [I Cor 15:48]. So then,
what is the image of the heavenly man? Listen to the divine Paul:
"He is the reflection of the glory and very stamp of the nature" and

the exact image of God the Father [Heb 1:3]. The Son is thus the icon of the Father, and the Holy Spirit the icon of the Son. Whoever, therefore, has seen the Son, has seen the Father, and whoever has seen the Holy Spirit has seen the Son. As the Apostle says: "The Lord is the Spirit" [II Cor 3:17]; and again: "The Spirit Himself intercedes for us with sighs too deep for words...crying 'Abba, Father' " [Rom 8:26 and 15]. He says rightly that the Lord is the Spirit when He cries "Abba, Father!" not that the Son is the Spirit—far from it!—but that the Son is seen and beheld in the Holy Spirit, and that never is the Son revealed without the Spirit nor the Spirit without the Son. Instead, it is in and through the Spirit that the Son Himself cries "Abba, Father!"

There is no cause for despair: believe, and you will see

Beloved, if you are ignorant of these things, do not throw yourself into despair and say: "I neither know these matters nor am able to learn them. Neither, again, have I the strength ever to ascend up to and attain the heights of this knowledge, and contemplation, and purity." Neither should you say: "Since, unless one becomes such a person and clothes himself with Christ as God from this moment, and looks wholly upon Him, and possesses Him dwelling within himself, he does not enter into His Kingdom, what use is it to me to struggle hard and be deprived even of the enjoyment of this present life?" Do not say this! Do not even think it! Please listen instead to my advice and, with the aid of the grace of the All-holy Spirit, I will tell you the way of salvation. First of all, then, believe with all your soul that everything I have said is true, is in accordance with the divine and God-inspired Scripture. Thus, everyone who believes in the Son of God is required to become such as I have described. He has given us power to become the sons of God and so, if we desire, there is nothing to hinder us. It is for this reason that the whole economy and condescension of the Son of God has come to pass: in order that, through our faith in Him and by keeping His commandments, He might make us sharers in His divinity and participants of His Kingdom. Indeed, unless you believe that this will truly occur, you will certainly not seek them out, and unless you ask, you will not receive it. "Seek," He says, "and you will receive; ask, and it will be given you" [Mt 7:7]. Believe, follow the holy Scriptures, and do whatever they tell you, and you will find everything without exception to be as it is written—and, in fact, you will find much more than is written in the Scriptures. What more? This: "What no eye has seen, nor ear heard, nor the heart of man conceived," those good things "which God has prepared for those who love Him" [I Cor 2:9]. If, as I have said, you firmly believe in these good things, then you as well will see them just as Paul did. And not only that, but you will hear ineffable speech and be caught up into Paradise. Which Paradise? The same that the thief entered into together with Christ, and where he is even now.

Do you want me to tell you what the good things are which eye has not seen nor ear heard, nor the heart of man conceived? I know that you long to hear about what he who saw them could neither utter nor interpret. Why could he not? In order that he not be disbelieved by his listeners. So, if you are not going to believe in what I am about to say, then stay right where you are! It is better that you not even glance with your mind's eye at the question before us. Because, if you do put aside what is said to you and refuse my words—rather, God's own words, since our words are from Him—the Word Himself will condemn you on the day of judgement. Listen instead to my words— or better, as I said, to God's words—without doubting, and learn from them the solution to this question as from one who states it clearly and with wisdom.

The vision of God and the Eucharist

I say that the ineffable speech which Paul heard spoken in Paradise were the eternal good things which eye has not seen, nor ear heard, nor the heart of man conceived. These things, which God has prepared for those who love Him, are not protected by heights, nor enclosed in some secret place, nor hidden in the depths, nor kept at the ends of the earth or sea. They are right in front of you, before your very eyes. So, what are they? Together with the good things stored up in heaven, these are the Body and Blood of our Lord Jesus Christ which we see every day, and eat, and drink. These, we avow, are those good things. Outside of these, you will not be able to find one of the things spoken of, even if you were to traverse the whole of creation. If you do want to know the truth of my words, become holy by practicing God's commandments and then partake of the holy things, and you will know precisely the force of what I am telling you. But, for further confirmation, listen to the words of the Lord Himself when He speaks thus to the Jews and to His own disciples:

> Truly, truly, I say to you, it was not Moses who gave you the bread from heaven; My Father gives you the true bread from heaven. For the bread of God is that which comes down from heaven and gives life to the world. They said to Him: Lord, give us this bread always. Jesus said to them: I am the bread of life; he who comes to Me shall not hunger, and he who believes in Me shall never thirst...The Jews then murmured at this, because He said I am the bread which came down from heaven. They said: Is this not the son of Joseph whose father and mother we know? How does He now say, I have come down from heaven? [Jn 6:32-35; 41-42]

So then, you must not be like the Jews as well, muttering and saying: "Is not this the bread on the diskos and the wine in the chalice which we see every day, and which we eat and drink? How does this man say that these are those good things which eye has not seen, nor ear heard, nor the heart of man conceived?" Listen instead to what the Lord said in reply to them:

> Do not murmur among yourselves. No one can come to Me unless the Father Who sent Me draws him; and I will raise him up at the last day. [Jn 6:44]

He says, as it were: "Why do you disbelieve and doubt this? No one can know My divinity—for this is the same as to come to Me—unless my Father draws him." In speaking of attraction, He makes it clear that there is no compulsion, but rather that He has invited through revelation those whom He foreknew and predestined, it being evident that He attracts them by virtue of their love for the One Who is thus revealed to them. This is indicated still more clearly in the following: "It is written in the prophets, 'And they shall be taught by God' "[Jn 6:45]. He who is taught by God is thus able to believe in the Son of God and, having learned from the Father, comes to Me. "Not that anyone has seen the Father except Him Who is from God; He has seen the Father" [Jn 6:46]. Again He says:

> Truly, truly I say to you, he who believes has eternal life. I am the bread of life. Your fathers ate the manna in the wilderness, and they died. This is the bread which comes down from heaven, that a man may eat of it and not die. I am the living bread which came down from heaven; if anyone eats of this bread he will live forever; and the bread which I shall give for the life of the world is My flesh. The Jews then disputed among themselves, saying; How can this man give us His flesh to eat? So Jesus said to them; Truly, truly, I say to you, unless you eat the flesh of the Son of Man and drink His blood, you have no life in you. He who eats My flesh and drinks My blood has eternal life, and I will raise him up at the last day. For My flesh is food indeed, and My blood is drink indeed. [Jn 6:47-55]

You have heard that the communion in the divine and immaculate mysteries is everlasting life, and that the Lord says He will raise up at the last day those who have everlasting life. This is not, certainly, that anyone else will be left in the tombs, but that those who have life will raised by the Life to life everlasting while the rest are raised to the eternal death of damnation. And, that this is the truth, listen to what follows:

> He who eats My flesh and drinks My blood abides in Me,

> and I in him. As the living Father sent Me, and I live
> because of the Father, so he who eats Me will live because
> of Me. [Jn 6:54-55]

Do you see what He is saying? The Son of God cries out plainly
that our union with Him through communion is such as the
unity and life which He has with the Father. Thus, just as He is
united by nature to His own Father and God, so are we united
by grace to Him, and live in Him, by eating His flesh and
drinking His blood. And, in order that we not think that everything is reduced to the visible bread, He says several times on
this account: "I am the bread which comes down from heaven."
Now, He did not say "Who came down", because this would
indicate that the "coming down" was a one-time event. What
then? He says, "Who comes down," clearly because He is
always and forever descending on those who are worthy, and
that this occurs both now and at every hour. And more: detach-
ing our minds from visible things, or better, leading us up
through them to the invisible glory of the divinity in His
Person, He says: "I am the bread of life" [Jn 6:48]; and again:
"My Father gives you bread not from the earth, but the true
bread from heaven" [cf. Jn 6:32]. When He said "the true bread
from heaven," He indicated that the bread of earth is false, that
it profits nothing.

Spiritual senses alone perceive the reality of the Eucharist

Now, in order to make this still more clear, He says: "The
bread of God is that which comes down from heaven, and gives
life to the world" [Jn 6:33]. Once more He says "comes down,"
and "gives life." Why this? So that you should suspect nothing
physical, nor conceive anything earthly, but instead see this bread
with spiritual eyes, and see that this little particle is made divine,
and has become altogether like the bread which came down from
heaven, which is true God, both the bread and drink of immortal
life; so that you should not be content with unbelief and with just

the visible bread which is perceived by the senses, and so not eat the heavenly, but only the earthly bread, and thus be deprived of life for not having eaten the heavenly bread in spirit. So Christ Himself says: "It is the Spirit which gives life; the flesh is of no avail" [Jn 6:63]. Whom, then, does it not profit? Those, He says, who say He is merely a man, and not God. Therefore, if you, yourself a believer, partake of mere bread and not of a deified body when receiving Him, the whole Christ Himself, how do you hope to take life from Him and with full awareness possess within yourself Him, the same Lord Who says: "He who eats the bread which comes down from heaven will live forever" [cf. Jn 6:58], and again: "The flesh avails nothing; it is the Spirit Who gives life"? It is the Spirit Who is really the true food and drink. It is the Spirit Who changes the bread into the Lord's body. [3] It is the Spirit Who really purifies us and makes us partake worthily of the body of the Lord. Those, on the other hand, who partake unworthily of the same, as the Apostle says, "eat and drink judgement upon themselves" as not discerning the Lord's body [I Cor 11:29].

Come therefore, as many as believe, as many of you as understand the power of the mysteries as we have explained it, as

---

3 Symeon is referring here to the *epiclesis* (invocation) of the Holy Spirit in the Byzantine Liturgy. In the present day service, as in Symeon's time, this prayer follows the "Words of Institution," and is/was believed to complete the consecration of the eucharistic gifts. The text from the Liturgy of St John Chrysostom, very little changed—if at all—from Symeon's day, is as follows: "Again we offer unto Thee this reasonable and blood-less sacrifice, and pray Thee and implore Thee, send down Thy Holy Spirit upon us and upon these gifts here set forth; and make this bread the most pure body of Thy Christ: Amen; and that which is in this cup the most precious blood of They Christ: Amen; making the change by Thy Holy Spirit: Amen, Amen, Amen." That the Spirit must descend "upon us" as well as upon the bread and wine is precisely the burden of St Symeon's argument here.

many as have eaten the heavenly bread, as many as from it and through it and in it and with it possess everlasting life, and, in this true life, let us all be caught up in the Spirit to the third heaven, or better, in spirit to the heaven itself of the Holy Trinity, so that, at once seeing and hearing, tasting and smelling and assuredly touching with the hands of our soul everything which has been said—and all that which remains ineffable—we may send up a hymn of thanksgiving to God and say: "Glory to You, Who have appeared and deigned to be revealed to and seen by us." Let us also say publicly to all our brothers: O fathers and brothers, monks and lay, rich, poor, slaves and free, young and old, and all of every age and race, listen to us!

Is God a liar? Or, if not a liar, is He powerless to do what He has promised? Is He late in visiting all the nations? Is anyone capable of hiding from His eyes? Is any man able to endure the revelation of His glory? No, of course not! For how, when "the heavens", as the Apostle says, "will pass away with a loud noise and the elements will be dissolved with fire" [II Pet 5:10] will a man endure then the day of His coming, of the God Who is unapproachable, Who dwells in light unapproachable, and Who comes in and with that light to the world so as to be seen by all flesh? Truly, great fear and trembling will then seize the sinners, and there will be nothing with which to compare their affliction, their pain and punishment.

Warnings to princes and prelates against the urge to rule

But, all you who believe and want to be saved, hear what the Holy Spirit says in the following:

Turn now, every one of you, from his evil way. [Jer 25:5]

Learn to do good and deliver the one who is wronged. [Is 1:17]

Seek God, and your soul shall live. [Ps 69:32]

Depart from evil, and do good. [Ps 37:27]

You kings! Desire to wear temperance, righteousness, mercy,

the true faith, rather than the crown and purple robe. You patriarchs! Unless you are friends of God, unless you are His sons, unless you are gods by adoption and, by the grace which is given us from above, are like Him Who is God by nature, leave your thrones and go take counsel first from the Holy Scripture and, when you have become a reflection of God, then you may touch with trembling the holy things. If you are not such, then on the day of His revealing you shall know that our God is a devouring fire—not, indeed, for His friends, nor for those who love Him, but for those who do not receive Him when He comes as light. You rulers and you rich! Join instead those who are ruled and the poor, since it is difficult for a rich man to enter the Kingdom of Heaven. And, if it is difficult for a rich man, how shall a ruler ever enter there? Not at all![4] For the Lord says to His disciples: "The rulers of the nations lord it over them, but it shall not be so among you. Whoever would be first among you, let him be last of all, slave of all, the servant of all" [cf. Mk 10:42-43].

Whom then does Scripture call a ruler? Someone who seeks his own honor, it says, who looks to fulfill his own will by ruling. If then our Lord and God came down upon the earth for our sake and gave us a type and pattern of salvation when He said: "I have come not to do My own will, but the will of the Father Who sent Me" [Jn 6:38], who could ever be saved among those who believe in Him who does not do His will, but fulfills his own? Obviously, no one possibly could. Why, indeed, am I even talking of his being saved, since such a person could neither be a believer nor a complete Christian? And Christ our God makes this clear when

4 A remark typical of Symeon's distrust of worldly power and wealth. The former, however, he understands as spiritually the more dangerous. Here we do not find merely the accents of someone who struggled for much of his life against the "establishment" of his day, but as well the echo of the whole spiritual and ascetic tradition of the Christian East.

He asks: "How can you believe"—that is, in Me—"who receive glory from one another and do not seek the glory that comes from the only God?" [Jn 5:44]. Therefore, no one who seeks the glory of God and hurries to do His will in every way and in every deed would ever by himself conceive of ruling anyone, or of lording it over small and great. Instead, the more people entrusted to his administration and care, so much the more would he come to perceive himself as the least of all and as a servant of those many people. On the other hand, those such as are not of this disposition, but are rather wholly possessed of a sense of human glory and have acquired an appetite for wealth and luxury, such people, I am sorry to say, are really gentiles and not true Christians, in accordance with the divine voice of Jesus, of God, Who says: "The gentiles seek all these things." But to you He adds, "Seek first the Kingdom of God and His righteousness, and all these things will be added to you" [Mt 6:32-33].

The reign of Christ begins NOW

But, do you understand which Kingdom it is that He says we are to seek? The one which is high up in Heaven, which is going to come after the general resurrection, which, as it were, is in some time and place far away—is it this Kingdom which He tells us to seek? Not at all! Then, which one is it that we are ordered to seek? Pay close attention to which Kingdom it is which we ought to seek. God, Who is the maker and creator of all things, reigns forever over everything in heaven, and on earth, and beneath the earth. However, He also reigns over what has not yet come to be, since in Himself it exists already and because whatever will happen later will happen through Him. No less does He reign over each one of us in justice and knowledge and truth. Thus, it is this reign which Christ tells us to seek, such that, just as Scripture says that "God reigns over the nations" [Ps 47:8], He should reign also over us since we are from the gentiles. But how will He reign? As mounted on us like on a kind of chariot, and as holding in His

hands the wills of our souls like reins. When He finds us docile,
He will lead us where He chooses, even to the fulfilling of His
will, and He will use our wills like steeds in voluntary submission
to His ordinances and commandments. Thus, indeed, does God
reign in those in whom He did not reign before, in those who are
in the process of purification through tears and repentance, and
who are being made perfect by the wisdom and knowledge of the
Spirit. So, too, do human beings become like cherubim in this
world, bearing aloft on the backs of their souls Him Who is God
above all. Who then would be such a fool, or so unfeeling, as to
desire power, or glory, or riches to the sight and experience of this
glory? Indeed, who would be so insane and foolish as to imagine
that any other glory, or kingdom, or wealth, or honor, or rule, or
luxury, or any other benefit said or thought to be on earth or in
heaven, could be greater than the Kingdom and glory of God, so
as to choose the first in preference to the second? Truly, there is
nothing else preferable to this for those who have any sense.[5]

Therefore, when Christ encompasses us and seeks to reign
over us, no one should be so stupid as to reject Him. No one, I feel,
should deprive himself of this great and welcome gift. No one should

5 God as mounted on the soul and directing it has several refer-
ents. In the Greek classical tradition one recalls, of course, the
charioteer of Plato's *Phaedrus* (246), an image which is taken
up in Christian spiritual literature especially by Evagrius of
Pontus (see our *Introduction*, forthcoming, volume III). On the
other hand, Symeon is quite as clearly looking here to the
scriptural image of God mounted upon the Cherubim in Ezekiel
1:4-28, and likely as well to the "Hymn of the Cherubim" sung
during the offertory of the Byzantine Liturgy which takes the
prophet's imagery and applies it to the assembled believers:
"Let us in mystery represent the Cherubim...that we may lift up
upon ourselves the King of all." The notion of the human soul
as "throne," "place," or "temple" of God seems also to be
involved. Here again, Evagrius is certainly one source for
Symeon, but the most important is assuredly the author of the
Macarian Homilies (cf. esp. *Homily* I.1-3 and 9).

abandon God, the giver of wealth and maker of all, for the sake of temporary riches. For the sake of passionate attachment to parents, to friends and relations, no one should deny the Master of the angels. No one should be deprived of the sweetness of that life which is real for the sake of fleshly appetite. No one should become a stranger to the eternal and unending glory for the sake of a glory which quickly fades. Instead, if it be possible, let us all come together for the same purpose. Let us all desire and strive that He, Who is above every rule and authority, and every name that is named, should come upon us and reign over each of us, so that each, receiving Him entire within, may possess Him inseparably both day and night, and may be radiant with the same unapproachable light which shall devour those who oppose Him when He comes for the unbelievers, those who now neither receive nor would have Him reign over them. Let us possess Him likewise on entering our houses, and lying down on our beds, at once both woven about with His unendurable light and by Him ineffably embraced. He consoles us in illnesses, chases sorrows and trials away, repels demons, provides us with joy by the hour and with tears that are sweeter than honey and beeswax. He heals the passions of soul and body, makes death vanish away, makes life well up inexpressibly within, and, on our departure from the body, draws each of us up into the heaven of heavens, and there, borne up mounted on our shoulders, He is received again whence He was never parted.

Beloved, you must experience and learn these things with the awareness of all your soul, so that you may have God to carry you up with Himself, now without your body but, later, He will raise it up as well and give it back to you as spiritual. He will reign over you for ages without end. He will carry you up into the air forever, and will be carried by you forever, Who is God above all, and to Whom is due all thanksgiving, honor, and worship, together with His Father Who is without beginning, and His All-holy, good, and life-creating Spirit, now and ever, and unto ages of ages. Amen

TENTH ETHICAL DISCOURSE

Introduction

Discourse X, on the "Day" of Judgement, continues the theme of the saints in light, particularly certain lines of thought sketched in the first two discourses: the Eighth Day, the Church, and the sacraments. Symeon wishes to defend the thesis that the saints in fact experience the "Day of the Lord" already in this life. The Day is nothing other than the manifestation of the glory of Christ's divinity. Christ is Himself "that Day" and, Symeon implies, He is at once the light of heaven and the fires of hell. When at the end He manifests Himself to those who have rejected Him, His glory will be terrible and burning. For the just, however, who have been led through repentance and the practice of the commandments to know their own sins and so be cleansed through tears, the "Day of the Lord" will never come as terror and burning because it lives in them already. From there he moves on to a consideration of the sacraments, Baptism and Eucharist. On the one hand, these are truly the means whereby the glory of God, the Holy Spirit, comes to "tabernacle"—a reference to John 1:14—in the Christian. They make us one with the risen body of Christ. On the other hand, the mere form of the sacraments does not suffice. We must perceive in faith the Holy Spirit at work in them, and such perception is given us only if we in our turn give evidence of faith by following the commandments. Without this living and conscious communion, we will find no salvation. Without it, and here Symeon harks back again to his use of John 6 earlier, we are no better than the Jews who refused to recognize Christ for what He was. He was "merely"

141

a man in their eyes. Similarly, Baptism and Eucharist will merely be water, bread, and wine for us if we remain unconscious of the Spirit Who is "ineffably mingled" with them. Those who deny the possibility of this conscious perception are once more excoriated. Symeon points to the example of the martyrs and, as a possibility open to everyone, of the ascetics. Both martyrs and ascetics sacrificed and labored because they knew that the "Day" of Judgment is now, not hidden at the end of time, and that we are called to know and reflect "the ineffable sea of divine glory" now as well. This is also the real meaning and content of the Eucharist. It is the glory present now. The discourse concludes with a series of "Beatitudes" in praise of those who see Christ in this life—though here, too, we find the all-important allowance made for those who do not see, but still strive. Symeon includes the wonderful image of the saint as the one who carries Christ within and knows His presence as a pregnant woman knows the child who stirs inside her womb. His last word is an exhortation to struggle with the passions and a warning that we have no excuse if we do not.

ON THE FEARFUL DAY OF THE LORD AND THE FUTURE JUDGEMENT

Beloved, there is much for us to say about the judgement, and the interpretation is difficult because it is not about things which are present and visible, but about future and invisible matters. There is therefore great need of prayer, of much effort, of much purity of intellect, both in us who speak and in those who listen, in order for the first to be able and know and speak well and for the others to listen with understanding to what is said. What then is the purpose of this discourse? Its subject is the great and manifest and fearful day of the Lord, and we write it in order to know why it is called and said to be the Day of the Lord.

The Day of the Lord is the full manifestation of Christ

It is not called Day of the Lord as being the last of these present days, nor because it is on this day that He is going to come again in the same way that we say for feast days of the present time the "Day of Pascha," or "Day of Pentecost," or the day on which the emperor is going to come out and do this and that. Neither is it called Day of Judgement because it is on this day that judgement is going to take place, since the day when this occurs is not other than the Lord Who will come on it, but it is called this because He Himself, the God and Master of all, will at that time shine with the glory of His own divinity. Even the physical sun will be hidden by the radiance of the Master and will become invisible, just as now the stars are eclipsed by the former and not seen. The stars will then be quenched and all visible things will be rolled up like a scroll, that is, they will give way and yield their place to the Master. And He alone will be at once "Day" and God. He Who is now invisible to all and dwells in light will then be revealed to all as He is, and will fill all things with His light, and will be without evening, without end, a day of everlasting joy, but absolutely unapproachable and unseen for those who, like me, are lazy and sinners. Because this did not happen while they yet lived, because they lacked zeal to see the light of His glory and, through purification, to have Him completely indwelling in themselves, He will also naturally be unapproachable for them in the future.

Summary of the creation, Fall and Incarnation

As holy Scripture says, God willed from the very beginning to make His own good ours as well. He bestowed free will on the first created couple, our ancestors, and through them on us. This was in order that, not from sorrow or necessity, but as moved by a favorable disposition they should follow His commandment and do it with joy. Thus they would be accounted as having acquired the virtues by their own efforts, in order to offer them up as their gift to the Master and so progressively be led up by them to the

perfect image and likeness of God, and approach the Unapproachable without suffering bodily death or the danger of being con-
sumed by His fire, and one by one, generation upon generation,
draw near to Him. But, since the first couple submitted first to the
will of the enemy and became transgressors of God's commandment, they not only fell away from the greater hope, which is to
say, from entering into the Light itself which neither fades nor has
an evening, but were changed as well into corruption and death.
They fell into lightless darkness and, becoming slaves to the
prince of the dark and ruled over by him, they entered through sin
into the darkness of death. Later we, too, who were born of them
stooped to the will of this tyrant and were enslaved. This did not
happen by compulsion, as is shown clearly by those who lived
before the Law and under the Law and were found as well-pleasing because they dedicated their own will to the Master, and not
to the devil. Then the Lord Who loves mankind, having willed to
redeem those who before and during the Law were well-pleasing
to Him, and to bestow by grace freedom on those who are after the
Law, and, so to speak, deliver everyone all at once who were
well-pleasing to Him before and during and after the Law, from
the devil's tyranny, He Himself, Who is able to do all things and
is beneficent, undertook to accomplish this work through Himself.
For the man whom He had made by His own invisible hands
according to His image and likeness He willed to raise up again,
not by means of another but by Himself, so that indeed He might
the more greatly honor and glorify our race by His being likened
to us in every respect and become our equal by taking on our
human condition. O what unspeakable love for mankind! the
goodness of it! That not only did He not punish us transgressors
and sinners, but that He Himself accepted becoming such as we
had become by reason of the Fall: corruptible man born of corruptible man, mortal born of a mortal, sin of him who had sinned,
He Who is incorruptible and immortal and sinless. He appeared in
the world only in His deified flesh, and not in His naked divinity.

Why? Because He did not, as He says Himself in His Gospels, wish to judge the world but to save it.

The merciful veiling of the light which is judgment and grace

The revelation of His divinity becomes in fact a judgement for those to whom it is revealed. No flesh could have endured the glory of His divinity as manifested naked of its joining and inexpressible union in the God-man. All creation would instead have been utterly destroyed both in body and soul, since at that time all were possessed by unbelief. For the divinity, which is to say the grace of the all-Holy Spirit, has never appeared to anyone who was without faith; and, if it were to appear by some paradox among men, it would show itself as fearful and dreadful, as not illumining but burning, not as giving life but as punishing dreadfully. And this is clear from the things which the blessed Paul, the vessel of election, suffered.[1] In the encounter with the radiance of the unapproachable light which flashed around him like lightning, his vision was wounded, and rather than being illumined he was darkened. He could not see, and lost even his natural faculty of sight. These things happened to him who would later become the great teacher of Christ's Church! That man who was so great, the same man who later said: "The God Who said 'Let light shine out of darkness' has shone in our hearts," and a little later: "We have this treasure"—i.e., of illumination—"in our hearts" [II Cor 4:6-7] could not at that time see even the least glimmer of the light.

From this lesson we therefore learn that grace, on the one hand, is unapproachable and invisible to those who are still possessed by unbelief and the passions, and is seen, on the other hand, and revealed to those who with faith and in fear and trembling do the commandments and give evidence of a worthy repentance. This same grace of itself incontestably brings the future judge-

1 Cf. Acts 9:3-18.

ment to pass in them. Rather, indeed, it becomes itself the day of divine judgement by which he who is purified is continually illumined, sees himself as he is in truth and in every detail, and all his works for what they are, whether done by the body or acted on by the soul. Nor this alone, but he is as well judged and examined by the divine fire, and, thus enriched by the water of his tears, his whole body is moistened and he is baptized entire, little by little, by the divine fire and Spirit, and becomes wholly purified, altogether immaculate, a son of the light and of the day, and from that point on no longer a child of mortal man. It is quite for this reason, too, that such a man is not judged at the judgement and justice to come, for he has already been judged. Neither is he reproved by that light, for he has been illumined beforehand. Nor is he put to the test and burned on entering this fire, for he has been tried already. Neither does he understand the Day of the Lord as appearing sometime "then," because, by virtue of his converse and union with God, he has become wholly a bright and shining day. Nor does he find himself then in or with the world, but is altogether outside of it. Thus the Lord says: "I chose you out of the world" [Jn 15:19], and the Apostle adds:

> but if we judged ourselves truly, we should not be judged. But when we are judged by the Lord, we are chastened, so that we may not be condemned along with the world [I Cor 11:31-32];

and again he says: "Walk as children of the light" [Eph 5:8].

The saints already live in that Day, but it is judgement for the reprobate

As many therefore as are children of the light also become sons of the Day which is to come, and are enabled to walk decently as in the day. The Day of the Lord will never come upon them, because they are already in it forever and continually. The Day of the Lord, in effect, is not going to be revealed suddenly to those who are ever illumined by the divine light, but for those who are in the darkness of the passions and spend their lives in the world hungering for the things of the world, for them it will be fearful and they will experience it as unbearable fire. However, this fire which is God will not appear in an entirely spiritual manner but, one might say, as bodilessly embodied, in the same way as, according to the Evangelist, Christ of old was seen by the Apostles after having risen from the dead. While He was being taken up into Heaven, the angels said to them: "He will come again in the same way as you saw Him go into heaven" [Acts 1:11]. Unless this were the case, how could the sinners, the unbelievers, the heretics and deniers of the Spirit see Him, those who are blind and the eyes of whose souls are stopped-up by the mire of unbelief and sin? It is just as Paul the Apostle wrote to the Thessalonians. When he spoke about those who had fallen asleep and the future glory, and about how the saints would be taken up into the clouds, he said:

> But as to the times and seasons, brethren, you have no need to have anything written to you. For you yourselves know well that the Day of the Lord will come like a thief in the night. When people say "there is peace and security," then sudden destruction will come upon them as travail comes upon a woman with child, and there will be no escape. But you are not in darkness, brethren, for that day to surprise you like a thief. For you are all sons of the light and of the day; we are not of the night or of darkness. So then, let us not sleep, as others do, but let us keep vigil and be sober. [I Thess 5:1-6]

and a little later he says:

> For God has not destined us for wrath, but to obtain salvation...so that whether we wake or sleep we might live with Him. [I Thess 5:9-10]

On hearing "sons of the light and sons of the day," beloved, do not say in your heart that as many of us as are baptized in Christ and believe in Him, and worship Him as God, have also been clothed with Him, and that we are all, completely without perceiving it, sons of the light and of the day and not of the night and darkness. Neither say nor imagine this, and then spend the rest of your days in negligence and carelessness, merely imagining and fancying yourselves to be something when in fact you are nothing. Instead consider and observe precisely what you are, and then say: "If all men who are in the world and who see this sun by the senses are blind, since I am obviously no more than the others, I, too, am together with them in darkness. For just as when the sun sets every day there is night and I see no more of it, so, too, when I die I shall not see light anywhere, but will be forever in lightless and sunless darkness, and never again will I see with my eyes this visible light. For men, once separated from the body, are separated from everything which is perceived by the senses. If I am therefore now in darkness, I shall also be in darkness after my death. Clearly, the Day of the Lord will also come upon me as a thief in the night, and as the pain which comes upon a woman giving birth, and I shall be unable to escape."

Sacramental forms and mere profession of faith are not enough

Our salvation is not by the baptism of water alone, but also by the Spirit. Neither is it by the bread and wine alone of communion that we receive the forgiveness of our sins and participation in life, but also by the divinity which mystically accompanies and is unconfusedly mingled with them. We say "mystically" because that divinity is not revealed to everyone, but to those who are worthy of everlasting life, and it makes them sons of the day and of the light who see it. Those who do not see the light, though it shines clearly, are rather instead the people who sit in darkness. Brothers, do not let anyone fool you with empty words; neither let anyone rejoice merely in his faith in Christ. For "Christ," he says, "if you be circumcised, will be of no advantage to you" [Gal 5:2]; and again: "Faith by itself, if it has no works, is dead" [Jas 2:17].

Just as the body without a soul is dead, so faith as well is dead without works. Those who confess that Christ is God and do not keep His commandments will not be reckoned merely as denying Him, but also as insulting Him. Nor this alone, but as even more than those who circumcise their bodies will they be justly condemned as mutilating God's commandments. How shall he be accounted a son who dishonors his father? How could he walk in the light as in the day who is separated from the light? Brothers, this is impossible!

If someone should say that no one is able to keep the commandments, let him know that he is slandering and condemning God as having ordered us to do what is impossible. This man will not escape the inevitability of justice but, like the man who said: "I knew you to be a hard man, reaping where you did not sow and gathering where you did not winnow" [Mt 25:24], so will he be condemned. He shall be likened to the serpent who said to Adam: "God knows that when you eat of the tree you will be like Him, for this reason He commanded you not to eat of it" [cf. Gen 3:4]. In effect, such a man calls God a liar and a deceiver, and filled with envy. A liar because while He said: "My yoke is easy and My burden is light" [Mt 11:30], this man declares that not only is it not light, but indeed unbearable. A deceiver because He came down and made us many promises without wanting to give us anything. And more: jealous at our salvation, He has ordered us to do and keep such things as are impossible for us to fulfill, in order that He may take advantage of this excuse to deprive us of His good things. But woe to those who say such things, unless they repent. Our Master and God has commanded nothing which is burdensome, nothing oppressive. On the contrary, all is at once light and easy. Believe me, I myself know the commandment of God is easy, and the attaining of both Him and His Kingdom. Let me illustrate this with an example.

We are like rebels forgiven by a gracious emperor

A certain man was serving a rebel, an opponent and enemy of
the emperor of the Christians. He accomplished many victories
and acts of courage against the latter's servants. While he was held
in great honor by the tyrant and his troops, he received messages
on several occasions from the emperor of the Christians that he
should come to him, and be with him, and be honored with great
gifts and reign with him. He, however, for some years did not
want to do so and increased his warfare against him still more
fiercely. One day, though, when he had come to doubt himself and
had become sorrowful, he decided to take flight and go alone to
the emperor, reasoning within himself as follows: "If indeed I
have not up to now obeyed the king who has been sending me
messages, yet I believe he will not count the delay and tardiness
of so many years against me who am now returning, because, as I
hear, he is compassionate and beneficent, and he will have compassion on me and fulfill everything which he has been promising
me." As soon as he had pondered these things in his heart, he put
them into practice. When he approached the emperor and embraced his feet, he wept and asked for forgiveness. Seized by
unexpected joy, that good emperor immediately accepted him,
wondering at his conversion and humility. The man, instead of
making bold as he had thought he would and demanding honors
for the love and trust he had proven to the emperor by abandoning
the rebel and approaching the other's kingdom, instead lies
mourning over his tardiness and the crimes for which he had
previously been responsible. Raising him up, the emperor "fell
upon his neck and kissed him" [Lk 15:20] all over his eyes which
had been weeping for many hours. Then, when he had ordered that
a crown and robe and sandals be brought out that were like the
ones he was wearing, he himself clothed his former enemy and
rival, and in no way reproached him for anything. And this is not
the whole tale, but day and night he rejoices and is glad with him,

embracing him and kissing his mouth with his own. So much does he love him exceedingly that he is not separated from him even in sleep, but lies together with him embracing him on his bed, and covers him all about with his own cloak, and places his face upon all his members.[2]

A personal testimony: there is nothing difficult in God's commandments

Such is also our own situation with respect to God, and I know that it is in just such a manner that the beneficent God welcomes and embraces those who repent, who, fleeing an illusory world and its rule, strip themselves naked of the affairs of this life in order to approach Him as King and God. It is not so difficult for some at least to abandon their native land and renounce friends and relatives and leave behind the wealth which perishes. For my part, I found nothing burdensome or grievous or weighty in taking flight to my God and Savior. To continue in this personal vein, which I did not want to do but which may be necessary in order for me to leave something good with at least a few among you, let me add that I found joy and happiness overflowing in me at the revelation and appearance of His countenance. For me that saying of Paul's was clearly fulfilled which says: "For this slight momentary affliction He is preparing for us an eternal weight of glory" [II Cor 4:17], and that one of David where he says: "You have given me room when I was in distress" [Ps 4:1]. From that point on I considered the sorrows and trials which have come upon me as nothing compared to the glory of Jesus Christ which is not in

2 Sometimes the saint's gift for images will exceed his discretion and good sense. This appears to be one such instance. We leave it in solely out of respect for the integrity of the text. It is, however, consistent with the New Theologian's use of nuptial imagery elsewhere—see our *Introduction*, part II, in volume III forthcoming. See also his warning against taking his metaphors in a literal, sexual sense: "Understand this spiritually, you who read, lest you be wretchedly defiled", *Hymn* 46, lines 29-31.

the future, but revealed to me now through the Holy Spirit. By the participation in and sharing of that glory I thought nothing of even those mortal illnesses and other, more intolerable pains which happen to men in their trials. I forgot every pain and sorrow of the body. Thus I understood at once that the burden of the commandments is light and the yoke of the Lord easy, and, believe me, my not finding any opportunity to die for His sake was an intolerable tribulation for me.

Therefore, my beloved brothers, abandoning everything let us run naked and, approaching Christ the Master, let us fall down and weep before His goodness, so that He, indeed, having seen our faith and humility, may like the emperor in our story—or rather, even more so—welcome and honor us, and adorn us with His own robe and diadem, and make us worthy celebrants of the bridal chamber of heaven. There is no comparison here with going from one mortal king to another, with entering upon the advantage of an earthly kingdom. Here we ascend from earth to heaven and are made worthy of an eternal joy and an everlasting kingdom. We become a co-heir and associate of God, not just a king but as well a god from God, and we rejoice with God forever and ever. Brothers, I beg you, let us not therefore prefer anything earthly and corruptible so that we fall away from Christ's glory and communion. Let us instead strive now, from this point on, to purify ourselves, to receive the pledges—rather, to acquire that One Himself Who is above all, and in all, and is Himself everything that is good.

Baptism alone is no guarantee, as Scripture bears witness

No one should say either that "I have received Christ myself from Baptism and possess Him." Let this person learn instead that not all who are baptized receive Christ through Baptism, but only those who are firm in the faith and have arrived at perfect knowledge, or indeed have prepared themselves by a prior purification and thus come to Baptism. Whoever searches the Scriptures will know this from the words and deeds of the Apostles, since it is written:

> Now when the Apostles at Jerusalem had heard that Samaria had received the word of God, then sent to them Peter and John, who came down and prayed that they might receive the Holy Spirit; for it had not yet fallen on any of them, but they had only been baptized in the name of the Lord Jesus. Then they laid their hands on them and they received the Holy Spirit. [Acts 8:14-17]

Do you see how not all who are baptized receive the Holy Spirit immediately? Have you learned from the Apostles that, while some believed and were baptized, they did not put on Christ through Baptism? For, had this been the case, they would not have afterwards needed prayer and the laying-on of the Apostles' hands, since in receiving the Holy Spirit they would have received the Lord Jesus. Christ is not one thing and the Spirit another. Who said that? God the Word Himself said it to the Samaritan woman: "God is Spirit" [Jn 4:24]. If Christ is God, He is Spirit by nature of His divinity, and whoever has Him has the Holy Spirit while in turn, whoever has the Spirit has the Lord Himself, just as Paul, too, says: "The Lord is the Spirit" [II Cor 3:17].

Brothers, we must therefore look at ourselves and examine our souls scrupulously to see whether or not we have received the Lord Jesus Who was proclaimed to us and have acquired Him within us, and this in order that, as John the Evangelist says, we may know whether we have received power from Him to become the children of God. So let each by all means pay attention to what the Holy Scripture says and examine himself, as we said, lest he deceive himself in vain and, fancying himself faithful, be found without faith, and, thinking he has the Lord in himself, depart from his body empty and be condemned as possessing nothing, and, deprived even of what he imagined he had, be cast into the fire. How then shall we know if Christ is in us, and how should we examine ourselves? By recounting the oracles of the divine Scriptures and placing them before our souls like mirrors, by these we shall judge our whole selves. But, let us take our discourse up to a still higher plane and, God granting me speech and opening up my unclean mouth, I shall somehow set out for you, my brothers, the mode of your examination. However, I beg you, do pay attention, for the discourse touches on matters which are fearful.

The prologue to John: *a witness to baptism in the Holy Spirit and to the Eucharist*

In the beginning was the Word, and the Word was with God, and the Word was God. He was in the beginning with God; all things were made by Him...In Him was life, and the life was the light of men. The light shines in the darkness, and the darkness has not overcome it. [Jn 1:1-15]

In saying these things the Evangelist makes clear the Undivided Trinity, calling the Father "God," the Son "Word," and the Holy Spirit "Life," which Three are also one Light shining in the darkness. What sort of darkness is it, then? Clearly, he says it is in the visible creation. For God Who is light and who shines is present everywhere and in everything. And when he says, "The darkness has not overcome it," he means that no spot of sin has ever approached Him at all, nor has the creation ever impeded Him from shining, nor has it known Him, nor discovered Him, nor been united with Him, nor has it seen Him. Therefore, reinforcing this idea in order to make it more clear, he adds:

That was the true light which enlightens every man who comes into the world. He was in the world, and the world was made by Him, yet the world knew Him not. [Jn 1:9-10]

From the beginning, he says, God was everywhere, giving life to every man coming into the world, and before He made the world He was in the world. How? Because all things pre-existed with Him and all were in Him. For, in the case of those who have not yet been born, it is not as if they did not exist, but they are one with God as if they had already come into being. Then, says the Scripture, when He made the world He was not separated from it by space, but was in it and the world did not know Him.

How then was He everywhere before making the world and, when He had made it, how was He shining in it without the world comprehending Him? Pay careful attention: God "Who is everywhere present and fills all things" was not, Scripture says, separated from it by location when He created this sensible world, but by the nature and glory of His divinity, it being evident that nothing created approached or comprehended Him at all. Indeed, being inseparable from all He is as clearly in all. "And no one knows Him", says the Lord, "except the Son and anyone to whom the Son chooses to reveal Him" [Lk 10:22]. The Son is therefore in the world and yet unknown by the world: "He came to His own, and His own did not receive Him" [Jn 1:11]. The Evangelist calls the world and those in the world "His own" both because He is their Creator and Master, and because He is related to them by the flesh. Do not therefore skip past what we have just said. Know instead that the Word Who is in the beginning with God and is God, and has the Life in Himself, and has made all things, and is the light which illumines all men, He Who is in the world before the world and Who made it and exists within it, came embodied into the world in order that to those who receive Him out of faith in God and who keep His commandments and take up His cross He might be revealed as God and known for what He is—now, indeed, partially, so far as each allows, but in the Resurrection more manifestly. So the Evangelist says:

> But to all who receive Him, who believed in His name, He gave power to become children of God; who were born, not of blood nor of the will of the flesh nor of the will of man, but of God. And the Word became flesh and dwelt among us...and we have beheld His glory, glory as of the

only Son from the Father, full of grace and truth. [Jn
1:12-14]

Behold! These words are the mirror of which I spoke to you
before. And consider with me the precise meaning of the Gospel
saying, how clearly it teaches us the signs by which the faithful
are known so that we may each recognize ourselves and our
neighbors. "As many as received Him," he says, meaning clearly
those who have confessed Him as God and not merely man, to
them He gave power through Baptism to become children of God,
having freed them from the devil's tyranny so that they might be
not merely believers but, if they should wish to follow His commandments, acquire holiness in addition to the working of the
commandments; as He says in another place: "Be holy, for I am
holy" [I Pet 1:16; Lev 11:44]; and again: "Be merciful, even as
your heavenly Father is merciful" [Lk 6:36]. Then, after saying
this, the Evangelist indicates the mode of adoption to sonship
when he says: "Who were born not of the blood nor of the will of
the flesh, nor of the will of man, but of God." "Birth" is what he
calls here the spiritual transformation which is effected and beheld
in the Baptism of the Holy Spirit, just as the Lord Himself—Who
does not lie—says in the following: "John baptized with water,
but...you shall be baptized with the Holy Spirit" [Acts 1:5]. Thus
by this Baptism the baptized become as light in the light, and they
know the One Who has begotten them because they also see Him.

That Baptism alone does not suffice us for salvation, but that
communion in the flesh of Jesus God and in His precious blood is
still more suited and necessary for us, listen to what follows: "And
the Word became flesh and dwelt among us." That by this phrase
he is indicating the communion of flesh and blood, listen to what
the Lord says here: "He who eats My flesh and drinks My blood
abides in Me and I in Him" [Jn 6:56]. For, once this has happened
and we have been baptized spiritually by the Holy Spirit, and the
incarnate Word has made His tabernacle as light in us by the
communion of His immaculate body and blood, then we have seen

His glory, glory as of the Only-Begotten of the Father. Once, He says, we have been born spiritually by Him and from Him, and He has tabernacled in us bodily and we have made our abode consciously in Him, then immediately at that moment, at the hour itself when these things have occurred, we have seen the glory of His divinity, glory as of an Only-Begotten from the Father, glory of such a kind as is clearly possessed by none other, neither angels nor men. Since One is God the Father, and One His Only-Begotten Son, then one is the glory of Both which is made known and revealed to all whom the Son wills, through the Spirit Who proceeds from the Father.

So, brothers, let each of you who has bent his mind to the force of these sayings see himself. If one has received the Word Who has come, if he has become a child of God, if he has been born not of flesh and blood alone, but also from God, if he has known the incarnate Word tabernacling in himself and if he has seen His glory, glory as of the Only-Begotten of the Father, then behold! he has become a Christian and has seen himself born again, and has known the Father Who has begotten him, not in word alone but by the work of grace and of truth. Brothers, let us abide in this mirror of truth, and let us remove ourselves from the hurtful and heretical teaching and supposition of those who say that the glory of the divinity of the Lord Jesus is not revealed even now in us who believe by the gift of the Holy Spirit, because the gift is given in the revelation and the revelation becomes actual in the gift. One does not, therefore, receive a Holy Spirit Who is not revealed and seen by the intellect, nor does he see a revelation unless he has been illumined by the Holy Spirit, nor can he be called completely a believer unless he has received God's Spirit. It is just as Christ said to the Samaritan woman:

> Whoever drinks of the water that I shall give him will never thirst; but it will become in him a spring of water welling up to eternal life. [Jn 4:14]

"Now this," says the Evangelist, "He said about the Spirit, which those who believe in Him were to receive" [Jn 7:39]. Do you see how those who do not have the Spirit acting and speaking in them are unbelievers? Because the Lord does not lie; because He committed no sin and deceit was not found in His mouth. If, then, He said He would give the Spirit to those who believe in Him, then those who do not have the Spirit are obviously not believers at heart.

If someone should say that each of us believers has received and possesses this Spirit without being aware of it, he blasphemes. He makes Christ a liar Who said: "It will become in him a spring of water welling up to eternal life"; and again: "He who believes in Me...Out of his belly shall flow rivers of living water" [Jn 7:38]. If, therefore, the spring is gushing forth, clearly the river which is coming out and flowing down is visible to those who see. But if, as those who think so say, these things are at work in us without our knowledge and we perceive none of them, then it is obvious that we shall neither receive any perception at all of the life everlasting which accompanies them and abides in us, nor shall we see the light of the Holy Spirit. On the contrary, we would remain dead and blind without feeling, both now and in the world to come. According to these people, our hope would become vain and our pursuit empty, since we would still be in death without having received any awareness of everlasting life.

The light is here and now: the example of the Forty Martyrs of Sebaste

This is not the case, however. It is not. Rather, what I have said often before I will also say again and will never stop saying it. The Father is light, light the Son, light the Holy Spirit, one light, timeless, invisible, unmingled, eternal, uncreated, without quantity, without lack, invisible, outside and beyond all things, yet which both is and is perceived by the intellect, which no one among men has ever seen before having been purified, nor ever received before having seen it. For while many have seen it, they have not all acquired it, just like many have seen the great treasure in the royal vaults and have gone away empty. While a divine light and illumination often comes in the beginning to those who are fervently repenting, it passes away immediately. If they give themselves up even to death itself and seek it with hard labor, presenting themselves to the Lord as worthy and blameless in every way, then at last they receive it again come back to them. If, however, they become a little lazy and take leave from throwing themselves into greater labors by loving their own souls, they become unworthy of so great a gift and do not enter, while still living in the body, into everlasting life. But, if not now, it is clear that neither will they enter into it after their departure from the world. For if he who received the one talent and hid it in the ground was condemned because he had not multiplied it, how much more will he not be condemned who did not even keep what he had received, but lost it by his laziness.

It is therefore right here and now that, as the whole God-inspired Scripture says, the festival takes place. The track is here, and right here are the crowns of earnest given to those who prevail in the contests, and here the first-fruits of shame and punishment become evident and manifest in those who fail. And look at the Forty Martyrs[3] and all the others who have given witness for Christ's sake in agreement with the witness of this, our discourse. For while those who were still in the frigid lake received their crowns from God's hand, he who fled to the bathhouse was immediately killed by its warmth and departed to everlasting fire. Eustratius, though, who was known for his virtue, said while under torture for Christ's sake: "Now I know that I am a temple of God and that His Spirit dwells in me. Depart from me, all you

---

3 The reference is to the Forty Martyrs of Sebaste, commemorated on March 9th. See our note 1 to *Discourse* VI, volume II, forthcoming.

workers of iniquity!"; and to the tyrant who was judging him he said: "If the perceptions of your mind were not altered and your soul not changed into the earthly by the leaven of the passions, I would have shown you that this crucified one is Savior and Redeemer and Benefactor." Do you see how faith without works is dead? Because before the saint had entered in the contest of martyrdom he had only faith and not the Holy Spirit in himself, but when he had demonstrated his faith from his works, then indeed he knew himself a temple of God and beheld His Holy Spirit with the eyes of his intellect, consciously, dwelling within him. What could be more clear than this testimony?

The martyrdom of asceticism is open to everyone

If some should say: "Those men were martyrs. They suffered for Christ, and how is it possible for us to become their equals?" We might say in reply to them: You yourselves, too, if indeed you want to, can suffer and be tormented for Christ's sake, and be a martyr every day just like those men were, and not only in the day, but at night, too, and at every hour. And how might this be? If you, too, rank yourselves in battle against the vicious demons; if you take your stand by continually opposing sin and your own will. While those stood up against tyrants, we hold against demons and the destructive passions of the flesh which day and night and at every hour tyrannically attack our souls and force us to do things which do not belong to piety and which anger God. Therefore, if we stand against these and do not bend the knee to Ba'al, nor are persuaded by the whisperings of the evil demons, nor serve the flesh by taking thought for its lusts, we shall in consequence be martyrs ourselves by contesting against sin, thus recalling the martyrs and the unbearable lashes they endured, and so ourselves also stand against the devil. Surely, by looking to their efforts and by thinking and groaning from our souls at how we are inferior to their struggles, we shall be made worthy of the same crowns as they—if not indeed in quantity, yet still in quality in accord with the goodness from on high which is God's. And, if we cannot equal them in boldness, we shall certainly at least equal them in our endurance and in our thanksgiving for the pains of our labors.

While they were saved by the works and toils of the games, we hope to be saved by the works and toils of asceticism, and all is by the grace and love for mankind of the Master: they from the sweat and agonies of martyrdom, we from the tears and agonies of ascesis; they from the shedding of their own blood, we from the cutting-off of our own will, and by remaining steadfast and keeping before us the sentence of death, and by expecting death hourly, readily stretching our necks out to die for every commandment of the Master rather than accepting its transgression by even the merest word. We ought, brothers, to despise the present life equally with them. Because it is not possible, not possible, for any of us to receive the incorruptible without having abominated the corruptible as dung, nor for us who cling to the transient to inherit eternal life, nor for him whose heart is dominated by the least little passion to possess Christ indwelling him by the tabernacling of the Holy Spirit.

Symeon's opponents condemned out of their own mouths

God, to repeat myself, my brothers, is light, as when He says Himself: "I am the light of the world" [Jn 8:12]. If then you say that He is light in His flesh, then once He ascended and was hidden, He was consequently parted and separated from His disciples and subsequently from us, and thus, according to you, the whole world has become darkness. If, however, you confess that He is the light of the world by virtue of His divinity, how can you say that you do not see Him while imagining that He is within you? If Christ is the light of the world, those who do not see Him are obviously blind; and if the Holy Spirit is also light—as He is indeed also light—how can you say you do not see Him and yet think that He is within you without your being aware of it? But, if you say the Spirit is concealed by the passions within you, so that

you know Him not, you are making out that the divine is circumcised and dominated by evil, because an evil will is evil even
without bodily sin. He who says, therefore, that in his heart he has
the light concealed by the darkness of the passions and invisible
to him, is saying that the light is ruled by the darkness, and he
declares the Holy Spirit a liar Who says: "The light shines in the
darkness, and the darkness has not overcome it" [Jn 1:5]. The
Holy Spirit says that the light is not overcome by the darkness, and
you say that it is hidden away in you by the gloom of the passions?
So, first know your own self, whoever you may be who say this,
because you are consciously sinning! Since you confess that the
darkness of the passions has become a veil over the light which is
within you, you have in the first place already indicted and
condemned yourself, because you know that you sit in darkness
and serve the passions and, having received the power to become
a child of God, which is to say of the light, and be called a son of
the day, you have been inactive and idle. You spend your life in
darkness, are unwilling to get up and do God's commandments
and chase away the cloud of the passions, but instead make light
of the One Who has come down from heaven for your salvation
and Who now lies in your filthy heart covered by slime.

For this reason the light speaks as follows: "Wicked servant,
from your own mouth I will judge you because, as you say, I came
and dwelt in you Who am unapproachable to the orders of angels.
You, knowing this, allowed Me to lie buried by the darkness of
your evils, just as you yourself say. And, while I was patient for
so many years, expecting your repentance and awaiting in addition the doing of My commandments, you did not, even to the end,
choose somehow to seek Me out, nor did you pity Me Who was
choked and cramped within you, nor did you allow Me to find the
drachma which I had lost—I mean you—because I was not allowed to take flame and see you and be seen by you, but was
perpetually concealed by the passions which are in you. Therefore, you worker of iniquity, depart from me to the everlasting fire

prepared for the devil and his angels; because I hungered for your repentance and conversion, and you gave Me no food; I thirsted for your salvation, and you gave Me no drink; I was naked of your deeds of virtue, and you did not clothe Me with them; I existed in the narrow and filthy and dark prison of your heart, and you did not wish to come visit Me and lead Me out to the light; you knew Me to be lying in the infirmity of your laziness and inactivity, yet you did not minister to Me by your good works and deeds. So, go away from Me!"[4]

The Day is Now—though only a drop in the sea of glory to come

Be sure that the Lord will say these things, and says them even now, to those who say they have the Holy Spirit in themselves, but that He is covered over and hidden by the darkness of their passions, and is not seen by the intelligible eyes of their souls. But to those who say that they know Him while admitting that they do not see the light of His divinity, He says the following: "If you knew Me, you would have known Me as light, for I am truly the light of the world." And woe to them who say: "When will the day of the Lord come?" and make no effort to grasp it. For the coming of the Lord has already taken place and is ever taking place in the faithful, and is at hand for all who desire it. If He is the light of the world and said to His disciples that He would be with us until the consummation of the age, then how, being with us, shall He come again? In no way! For we are not sons of the darkness and of the night, that the light should take us by surprise, but are sons of the light and of the Lord's day. Therefore while we are yet alive we are in the Lord, and dying with Him we shall also live with Him, just as Paul says [Rom 14:8]. About this St Gregory the Theologian also says: "What the sun is to sensible things, so God is to things intelligible."[5] For He will be both the age to come

4 Cf. Mt 25:31-46 and, for a similar use of this text, *Catecheses* IX, esp. 26-60 (deC, 150-151).
5 Gregory of Nazianzus, *Or.* 14.8; *PG* 36.69A.

and the day without evening, bridal chamber and bed, land of the
meek and divine paradise, king and servant; just as He Himself
has said:

> Blessed are those servants whom the Master finds awake
> when he comes; truly, I say to you, he will gird himself and
> have them sit at table, and he will come and serve them.
> [Lk 12:37]

Therefore all these things, and others yet more which it is not
possible for a man to list, will Christ become for those who believe
in Him. Nor will this be only in the age to come, but first in this
life, then later in the future age as well. And if here more obscurely
and there more perfectly, still the believers do see plainly and
receive here-below, already, the first fruits of all that is beyond.
For while they do not receive all the promises here-below, yet
neither do they remain without any portion or taste of the things
to come by hoping for everything there and merely existing here.
Rather, since it is indeed through death that God arranged to give
us the kingdom of the Resurrection, and incorruptibility and all of
life everlasting, yet we are already, without a doubt, become in
soul partakers and communicants here-below of the future good
things, are as it were incorruptible and immortal and sons of God
and sons of light and of the day, heirs of the Kingdom of Heaven.
We clearly carry it around within us, because it is right here
already that we receive it all by the perception and knowledge of
our soul, unless we are in some respect untried with respect to our
faith or lacking in our keeping of the divine commandments. In
the body, however, we do not yet receive it. Just as Christ God
before His resurrection, we carry around our body as corruptible,
and, encompassed and bound by it with respect to our soul, we
cannot now accommodate receiving the entire glory which has
been revealed to us. In reflecting that ineffable ocean of glory , we
believe we see a single drop of it, and for that reason say that for
the moment we see as in a mirror and obscurely [I Cor 13:12], yet
we do see ourselves spiritually as like Him Whom we see and

Who sees us even in this present life. After the Resurrection, though, just as He Himself raised His own body from the tomb transformed by His divine power, so shall we, too, all receive our body as itself spiritual, and, having first been likened to Him in our soul, we shall then become like Him in both soul and body. This is to say that we shall be like Him, human beings by nature and gods by grace, just as He Himself is indeed God by nature Who in His goodness has taken on the nature of man. How must those who have accurately understood this mystery long for and desire death! As the Apostle says: "For while we are still in this tent, we sigh with anxiety [II Cor 5:4], awaiting the revelation of the sons of God" [Rom 8:19].

If this is not true, then Christ is only a prophet and the Eucharist merely bread

Indeed, if this is not the case and we do not enter into participation and communion with the eternal good things while yet in the body, and if we, the elect, do not receive grace, then Christ Himself is in fact a prophet, and not God. Everything which His Gospel says becomes instead a prophecy about the future and not a gift of grace. Similarly as well, the Apostles were entrusted with a prophecy, but not a fulfillment of what was prophesied, nor did they receive anything nor transmit anything to others. But, O! the ignorance and darkness of those who hold this view! According to them, it follows that our faith is comprised of empty words and devoid of deeds. Because, if the saving grace of God has shone on all men by word alone and not in reality, and if it is thus that we think the mystery of our faith has been accomplished, who is more wretched than we are? If Christ is the light of the world, and God, but we believe that no one among men sees Him continuously, who then is more faithless than we?

If He is light, therefore, but we say that those who are clothed with Him do not perceive Him, in what respect do we differ from a corpse? If He is the vine and we are the branches, unless we clearly know our union with Him, we are soulless wood, fruitless and withered, matter which is fit for the unquenchable fire. And if those also who eat His flesh and drink His blood have eternal life, according to His own word, but we in eating these perceive nothing more happening in us than the material food, nor receive in knowledge another kind of life, we then partake of mere bread alone and not also of God. For if Christ is God and man, His holy flesh is not flesh alone, but flesh and God inseparably yet without confusion: visible in the flesh, that is, in the bread, for physical eyes while invisible in its divinity for those same eyes, yet seen by the eyes of the soul. Thus He also says elsewhere: "He Who eats My flesh and drinks My blood, abides in Me and I in him" [Jn 6:56]. And He did not say that He abides in them and those in Him, but "in Me," which is to say, in My glory, My light, My divinity. Therefore He says: "I am in My Father and the Father in Me, and you in Me and I in you" [Jn 14:20]. So, if we think that all those things take place in us without our knowledge and awareness, who could adequately grieve for our lack of feeling? Truly, no one.

Beatitudes: blessed are they who see and struggle now

Blessed are they, however, who have received Christ coming as light in the darkness, for they are become sons of light and of the day.

Blessed are they who even now have put on His light, for they are clothed already with the wedding garment. They will not be bound hand and foot, nor will they be cast into the everlasting fire.

Blessed are they who have seen the same Christ while in His body, but thrice-blessed are they who have seen Him intelligibly and spiritually and have worshipped Him, for they will not see death forever. And do not doubt this when you see what happens on earth, for those condemned who are allowed to see the earthly emperor are immediately freed from the sentence which leads to death.

Blessed are they who daily feed on Christ with such contemplation and knowledge as the prophet Isaiah fed on the burning coal, for they are cleansed of every stain of both soul and body.

Blessed are they who hourly taste of the ineffable light with the mouth of their intellect, for they shall walk "becomingly as in the day" [Rom 13:13], and spend all their time in rejoicing.

Blessed are they who have recognized already here-below the light of the Lord as He Himself, for they shall not be ashamed when they appear before Him in the age to come.

Blessed are they who live always in the light of Christ, for they are and shall ever be His co-heirs and brothers both now and forever.

Blessed are they who have kindled the light in their hearts even now and have kept it unquenched, for on their departing this life they shall go radiant to meet the Bridegroom, and go in with Him to the bridal chamber bearing their lamps.

Blessed are they who have not reasoned in themselves that men in this life have no assurance of salvation but receive on their departure from it or, indeed, after it, for they have struggled to receive it now.

Blessed are they who have not hesitated at anything said here or suspected it to be false, for they, even if they possess none of these things (which I pray is not the case), yet at least they strive to possess them.

Blessed are they who seek with all their soul to come to the light, despising all other things, for, although they may not succeed in coming to the light while yet in the body, still in all likelihood they shall pass away with firm hopes and, though it be little, yet shall they enter into it.[6]

Blessed are they who ever weep bitterly for their sins, for the light shall seize them and change the bitter into sweet.

Blessed are they who shine with the divine light and who see their own infirmity and understand the deformity of their soul's

6 A second time that Symeon offers an important qualification of his normal insistence on the conscious perception of grace. See our note 1 to *Discourse* VII, volume II, forthcoming.

vesture, for they shall weep without failing and, by the channels of their tears, be washed clean.

Blessed are they who have drawn near the divine light and entered within it and become wholly light, having been mingled with it, for they have completely taken off their soiled vesture and shall weep bitter tears no more.

Blessed are they who see their own clothing shining as Christ, for they shall be filled hourly with joy inexpressible and shall weep tears of astounding sweetness, perceiving that they have become themselves already sons and co-participants of the resurrection.

Blessed are they who have the eye of their intellect ever open and with prayer see the light and converse with it mouth to mouth, for they are of equal honor with the angels and, dare I say it, have and shall become higher than the angels, for the latter sing praises while the former intercede. And, if they have become and are ever becoming such while still living in the body and impeded by the corruption of the flesh, what shall they be after the Resurrection and after they have received that spiritual and incorruptible body? Certainly, they shall not be merely the equals of angels, but indeed like the angels' Master, as it is written: "But we know," he says, "that when He appears we shall be like Him" [I Jn 3:2].

Blessed is that monk who is present before God in prayer and who sees Him and is seen by Him, and perceives himself as having gone beyond the world and as being in God alone, and is unable to know whether he happens to be in the body or outside the body, for he will hear "ineffable speech which it is not lawful for a man to utter" [II Cor 12:14], and shall see "what no eye has seen, nor ear heard, nor the heart of man conceived" [I Cor 2:9].

Blessed is he who has seen the light of the world take form within himself, for he, having Christ as an embryo within, shall be reckoned His mother, as He Himself Who does not lie has promised, saying: "Here are my mother and brothers and friends."

Who? "Those who hear the word of God and do it" [Lk 8:2]. So those who do not keep His commandments deprive themselves voluntarily of so great a grace, because the thing was and is and will be possible, and has happened and happens and will happen for all who fulfill His ordinances.

Christ is in the blessed like an infant within the womb

In order not to stop at the last without any witness and be suspected of speaking from ourselves and laying down as dogma that what is impossible is possible, let us once again introduce the blessed Paul himself, the mouth of Christ, into your midst. He makes our point clearly when he says: "My little children, with whom I am again in travail until Christ be formed in you" [Gal 4:19]. Now then, where or in what place or part of our body does he say that Christ takes form? Do you think he means on the brow, or in the face, or in the breast? Assuredly not! It is rather inside, in our hearts. Perhaps you supposed that He takes form bodily? Away with the notion! Rather, He indeed takes form, but bodilessly and as is proper to God. Besides, just as a woman surely knows when she is with child that the babe leaps in her womb and could never be ignorant of the fact that she has it within her, so the one who has Christ take form within himself and is aware of His stirring, which is to say His illuminations, is in no way ignorant of His leaps, that is His gleamings, and sees His formation within himself. Christ is not, for example, reflected like the light of a lamp in a mirror, is not an apparition without substance like the reflection, but appears in a light which is personal and substantial; in a shape without shape, and a form without form He is seen invisibly and comprehended incomprehensibly.

Avoid the least hesitation

Thus it is, my brother, that the incomprehensibility of our faith is comprehended. Thus it is for whomever the Father and the Son in the Holy Spirit come and truly make Their abode, in whom

They are beheld and comprehended unambiguously and without change, in whom They are known, as we have said, in one single light. Moreover, it is like someone chasing after a fugitive, even if he thinks he is close to him, at his heels, and it seems he is just about to touch him and brush him with his fingertips, yet cannot quite get hold of him and misses him, as they say, by a hair; so likewise neither, if there is some thought or reservation—I mean of unbelief, or double-mindedness, or fear—or if we hold on in negligence or sloth to some kind of passion, or at all hold out for the least little thing, we will not become partakers of divinity, nor be led up to the height of this glory. Just as in the case of the fugitive it was "by a hair," so does this "little thing" apply in spiritual matters. And if we do not perfectly, as if called to martyrdom, despise both our soul itself and our body, and give ourselves up completely to every kind of torment and death, and do not call to mind anything proper to the life and sustenance of this corruptible body, nor in fact care about anything, we shall not become friends and brothers, co-participants and co-heirs in contemplation and knowledge and experience, of the mysteries of God concerning which we have spoken.

For this reason, he who has not been made worthy to attain to these things and enter into possession of such great good things, let him at least know himself and not say, looking for excuses for his sins, that this thing is impossible or that, while it does happen, it does so without our knowing it. Instead, let him know, assured by divine Scripture, that this is, on the one hand, both possible and true, and, on the other, that it is by negligence and lack of the commandments that each man deprives himself in proportion of such great good gifts. To which may all of us attain, tasting here-below and knowing that the Lord is God, and seeing Him there entire and rejoicing with Him for ages of ages without end. Amen.

FOURTEENTH ETHICAL DISCOURSE

Introduction

Discourse XIV, on "the Feasts and Holy Communion," again goes back to the themes of the first discourses, in particular the Church as body of Christ and new creation, the "anatomy" of the virtues given in *Discourse* IV (volume II, forthcoming), and the Eucharist. Weaving these elements together is the unspoken assumption that the human being as microcosmos, a little world, reflects and embodies the greater world, macrocosmos, of the Church. Thus Symeon can warn his readers against taking the outward celebrations of the Christian feasts in splendidly adorned temples as the true feast, but rather as "symbol of the feast." Unless the visible and outward splendors indicate invisible and inward spiritual realities known and experienced by the believer, they are in vain and will leave one afterwards even worse off than before. In passages which recall Dionysius the Areopagite, Symeon suggests that the lights, incense, choirs, crowds of exalted guests and sumptuous refreshments of a solemn feast—presumably such as he would himself have celebrated at St Mamas or the great feasts and in memory of Symeon the Pious—should signify, respectively, the lamps of the virtues within the soul, the intelligible fragrance of the Holy Spirit, the festal and eternal assembly of the angels, the company of the saints, and the living bread of the Eucharist. Turning to the latter, he repeats what he has said on several occasions above, that only those who partake of the sacrament "in perception and knowledge," who see Christ with

the eyes of the intellect, can be said truly to commune in Him.
He concludes by exhorting his readers to commune worthily
and so share in the one, true feast, the eternal Pascha.

ON THE FEASTS AND THEIR CELEBRATION

The man who has been capable of understanding and is becoming aware that he entered naked into the world, this man will
recognize the One Who made him and will fear Him alone, and
will love and serve Him with all his soul and in no way prefer
any visible thing to Him, but, knowing himself with all certainty to be a stranger to everything on earth—and, one might
say, to everything in heaven as well—he will dedicate the
whole intent of his soul to the service of his Creator. For, if he
is a stranger to that from which he was formed and in which he
passes his life, so much the more will he be a stranger to those
beings from which he is far removed by nature and essence and
way of life. And, he who recognizes himself as being a stranger
to what is on earth, and who knows that he has come naked into
this theater and is going to leave it naked again, how will he
not mourn? How will he not weep, not only for himself, but for
all men who are of the same race and share the same suffering
with him? He, too, who loves and fears God alone, how will he
rejoice in the body or, in the way of men, somehow ignorantly
and irrationally celebrate feasts in the body when the Lord
Himself is ever saying to such as are faithful:

> The world will rejoice, you will be sorrowful...but be of
> good cheer, I have overcome the world [Jn 16:20,33]. [For
> I shall rise again in you], this lesser world having been
> swallowed up by the life which is awarded to all by My
> Spirit [cf. II Cor 5:4]; and when you have seen Me, your
> hearts will rejoice, and no one will take your joy from you.
> [Jn 16:22]

Vanity of purely outward ceremonial

How, then, can he who sees the heavenly Master ever enter into lust for any earthly thing, or conceive of anything which is not pleasing to God? Or how shall he who knows himself assuredly as naked and poor, even if he should possess everything—to speak in the manner of the Apostle [cf. II Cor 6:10]—take pride in beauty, or exalt himself in what he does now, or pay great attention to a multitude of candles and lamps, or fragrances and perfumes, or an assembly of people, or a rich and elaborate table, or boast in the appearance of friends or the presence of men who are glorious upon the earth? Of a certainty, he will in no way do so! Because he knows that everything and everyone is here today and tomorrow gone. Whatever is present today disappears after a little while. Nor does such a man, while he knows how to celebrate a feast well, fix either his mind or his perception at all on what is taking place—for this is characteristic of those who imagine there is nothing beyond what is seen—but, as it were, he sees wisely with his intellect the future events which are present in the rites being celebrated. It is in them that his heart rejoices, and it seems to him that he is at once wholly with those future events and together, in the Holy Spirit, with those who celebrate the feast in heaven. He looks neither to the lights, nor the crowd of people, nor the gathering of friends, but thinks continually of what will happen a little later: the lights will be extinguished, each of his friends will leave for home, and he himself will be left alone in darkness.

Do not, therefore, reckon up the numbers of years and months and periods of time, nor tell me: "See, I have celebrated Christ's Birth, the Meeting at the Temple, Theophany, the Resurrection, the Ascension, the descent of the Spirit at Pentecost." Do not talk to me about these things, nor count up all the feasts, nor especially think that these suffice for your soul's salvation, nor imagine that the feast consists for you of brilliant robes, the proud steeds of the nobles, and expensive perfumes, nor of candles, lamps, and a crowd of people. These things do not make the feast radiant, nor are they the true feast, but are symbols of the feast. Beloved, what does it profit me, not just to speak of lighting candles and lamps in the church, but even if I were able to acquire such lights as the sun which shines from heaven, or instead of many lamps were to affix stars to the ceiling of the church and make it a new sky and a thing unheard of upon the earth, and again, in addition to this, if while rejoicing in this I were to be marveled at and praised by the assembled people—what would it profit me if, after a little while, after all the lights had been extinguished, I were myself to be left behind in the darkness? Or, too, if I were to perfume myself and the assembly with perfumes today, yet tomorrow be filled with the stink of my own flesh and its filth, where is my advantage? Tell me, you who take pride in splendid feasts and, if you have understanding as the wise man says [cf. Sir 5:12], answer me intelligently. If today I am illumined and tomorrow darkened, or rejoice today and grieve tomorrow, or enjoy health on this day and on the following one am plunged into illness, where is my gain? Tell me! What joy is there in what we have described?

"I have not chosen these feasts," says the Lord. "Who," He asks, "has required these things from your hands?" [cf. Is 1:11ff]. Christ did not lay down a law for us to celebrate feasts in this way. Then why do it? Let me first present you with the objections of those who resist my reasoning and say as follows: "What then? Shall we not light candles and lamps? Shall we not offer perfumes and incense? Should we not invite people to sing, nor gather acquaintances and friends and notables? Is this what you are saying? Is this your decree?" I do not say this, God forbid! On the contrary, I indeed both advise and encourage you to do these things, and to do them lavishly. Only, I want you to know the way you should do so, and will suggest to you here the mystery of the feast of the faithful. What do the things you do in types and symbols really mean?

The meaning of the symbols: lights, fragrances, crowds[1]

The lamps' underlying meaning is to show you the intelligible light. Just as this most beautiful house, the temple, is lit by the many lamps, so the house of your soul, more precious than this house, ought to be lighted and illumined intelligibly, ought to be burning with all the splendid virtues which are manifested in you because of the divine fire, such that there is no place left in you without its portion of light. The multitudes of lamps burning with visible fire provide you with a sketch of those thoughts which are in the form of light, so that, just as with material lamps, each should shine and no dark thought be left behind in the house of your soul, but all are bright throughout, burning ever with the fire of the Spirit, such that there is no break in the circle, like a corona,[2] of your discernment of the thoughts. The intelligible myrrh you find indicated by the outpouring of the perfumes and the composition of the incense. The latter also teach that you must acquire that myrrh abundantly for yourself. For the spiritual man that which is sprinkled on the outside will be an image of the dew which descends on Mt Zion, and as the oil which ran down the beard of Aaron, down to the borders of his robe [Ps 133:2].[3] But

1 The whole sequence of symbols here—lights, fragrances, crowds, the Eucharist—together with its reference to the inner life, recalls Dionysius Areopagita's *Celestial Hierarchy* I.3 (121D; Heil/Ritter, 8,21-9,6; Eng. Trans. Liubheid, 146) so closely as to comprise in our view an instance of direct influence.

2 By "corona" Symeon appears to have in mind an article of ecclesiastical furniture still found in Orthodox (esp. monastic) churches today. It is a large hoop or wheel-like object, of brass or wood, hung from the church's roof. A heavy chandelier is suspended so that it hangs in the middle of the corona. On great feasts, the lamps/candles of corona and chandelier are lit and both are set swinging. The resulting double motion and simultaneous play of light is intended to recall the celestial dance of the angels, and, with them, of all creation.

3 The "oil running down the beard of Aaron... etc.," *Ps* 133:2, is used in the Byzantine rite today in the vesting prayers said by

that which wells up from within and refreshes the spirit like water
will be like a spring overflowing with the waters of everlasting life
for him who is moved by the divine Spirit, and it takes fire and
rises like sweet-smelling smoke. It also shines brightly and
anoints the senses with spiritual perfume. It is as light and is
visible to those who are pure of heart. It is as a tree of life
crucifying the wills of the flesh, making everything fragrant and
ever gladdening the faithful with spiritual joy.

But the symbols do not consist merely in what we have said so
far. They also carry another reflection of spiritual teaching. For, if
God has thus adorned what is soulless with fragrance and has
glorified it, think how much more He will adorn you, if you choose,
with the forms of the virtues and glorify you with the fragrance of
the Holy Spirit—you, whom He made according to His own image
and likeness. These aromatics, put together by human hands and
perfuming your senses with the fragrance of the scented oils, depict
and, as it were, suggest your own creation by the art of their
making. Because, just as the perfumers' hands fashion the blended
perfumes from different essences and the product is one essence
out of many, so, too, did God's hands fashion you, who are
cunningly composed and combined with the intelligible elements
of the spiritual perfume, that is to say, with the gifts of the life-creating and all-efficacious Spirit. You, too, must give off the fragrance of His knowledge and wisdom, so that those who listen to
the words of your teaching may smell His sweetness with the
senses of the soul and be glad with spiritual joy.[4]

the officiating priest(s) prior to the Eucharist. This particular psalm
verse is recited while the cleric is donning the priestly stole (*epitra-
chelion*). Assuming the same association in Symeon's day, could
this be an allusion to the priestly character of each Christian?

4 The myrrh or fragrances here—which may apply to the incense
burned at the festal service—somewhat recalls Dionysius Areopagita on the divine myron (cf. *EH* IV.3, 4; *PG* 477D-480A),
though in Dionysius' case the reference is to Christ and the
union in Him of God and man.

The crowds which you have assembled to sing praises to God with loud voices give you a hint of the heavenly choirs and the innumerable angelic powers who sing the praises of the heavenly Master at your salvation. The praise and song which the first sing in harmony suggest that mystical hymn which the holy angels ceaselessly raise on high, such that you, too, may make of yourself such a one and, as an angel upon the earth, sing praises mystically and unceasingly to the God Who made you with the immaterial mouth of your heart. The friends and acquaintances and the presence of the officials teach you through their presence that you must become one who is counted among, and with a way of life similar to the Apostles, prophets, martyrs and all the righteous, by working all of the commandments and acquiring the wealth of the virtues.

If you think that this is the way you are celebrating the feasts, and that you have become such a one as our discourse has depicted, then in what you do you are celebrating a spiritual feast and are concelebrating with the heavenly powers of the angels. If, however, you are not, and if you will not make yourself such by doing the commandments, then what profit is there in your celebrating? There is fear lest you, too, hear like the Jews of old: "I will turn your feasts into mourning, and your joy I will turn into sorrow" [Am 8:10].

Our feasts are a type of the true feast: the light of the Holy Spirit

What then? You ask: "Should we not then celebrate the feasts with the body and the senses unless we are able to become such as your discourse has shown us?" But of course you should! "Keep your feasts," says Scripture [Nah 1:15], and perform what is to God's honor and His saints' as far as you are able, and invite everyone—kings, officials, bishops, clergy, monks, and laymen—so that God may be glorified through you, and their glory, as offered up to God by you, will be to your credit and you shall be acceptable to God. However, do not imagine that by glorifying

God and His saints here-below you make any kind of addition to their glory. How is that? Because the Apostle says: "What once had splendor has come to have no splendor at all, because of the splendor that surpasses it" [II Cor 3:10], and neither do the saints have any need of an earthly and human glory. Celebrate the feast instead that you may obtain mercy from God for honoring them, but do not then surmise that what you do is the true feast. Think of it rather as a type, and shadow, and symbol of that feast. For what communion, tell me, would what is sensible and without soul and in every way without a share in perception ever have with what is intelligible and divine and endowed with soul, or, put better, is spiritual and living and productive of everlasting life?

You who celebrate rationally and devoutly, let your feast not be the light which after a little while is extinguished, but let it be the pure shining itself of your soul, the knowledge of divine and heavenly things provided by the Lord to the man who in his intellect is a true Israelite. Let this light shine in you all your life, shine more than the sun's rays on all who are in the house of the world. Let it be the pure light of the world salted with the salt of the Spirit, and so be in accord with that commandment which decrees: "Let your light so shine before men, that they may see your good works, and give glory to your Father Who is in heaven" [Mt 5:16].

Instead of many lamps, let your thoughts be in the form of that light by which the whole world of the virtues is completed, and the ornament of the spiritual temple and its beauty is shown forth in radiance to those who see aright.

Instead of perfumes and aromatics, let the intelligible perfume of the Holy Spirit make you fragrant, whose savor is ineffable, and whose rising like smoke is as the scent of light.

Instead of a crowd of people, let the ranks of the holy angels come together with you and glorify God on your behalf and rejoice always in your salvation, and your ascent, and your progress.

Instead of friends and officials and emperors, let all the saints who are honored and venerated by them celebrate the feast and commune with you as friends. Let these be loved by you and preferred before anyone else, so that they may welcome you on your departure from this life to their everlasting tents, as Abraham received Lazarus the beggar into his bosom (though we have interpreted this text differently elsewhere).[5]

Instead of a table filled with an abundance of food, let yours be the living bread alone—not that which is perceptible and visible, but He Who comes and is given to you in and through what is perceptible, Who is Himself the bread which comes down from heaven and gives life to the world, and of Whom those who eat are not merely nourished, but are quickened and live as though they are raised from the dead. Let this be your unceasing and inexhaustible food and drink. And, as for wine, let it not be this visible wine, but that which appears as wine yet is perceived by the intellect as the blood of God, as light inexpressible, ineffable sweetness, everlasting joy. If you always drink this worthily, you shall never thirst—only, drink it with perception of soul, with your soul's powers prepared and at peace.

On the true bread, and on worthy and unworthy communion

Now, consider with me the thrust of what I have been saying. If you partake of such things with perception and knowledge, you do so worthily. If not thus, however, you certainly eat and drink unworthily. If it is with a pure contemplation that you have partaken of what you took, behold! you are become worthy of this table. If you have not become worthy, you will not be joined, you will in no way be united with God. Let those who partake unworthily of the divine mysteries not imagine then that they are simply joined by them and united to the invisible God. This will not happen to them at all, nor will it ever happen. For only those who

5 I confess I do not know the work to which Symeon is referring here.

by participation in the Lord's divine flesh, and who are judged worthy of the revelation of the invisible divinity through the actual contact with it of their intellect, who see and eat with their intelligible eyes and mouth, know that the Lord is good. They do not merely eat visible bread visibly, but at once eat and drink God as well with their intellect, feeding at the same time with a double perception on that which is both perceptible and intelligible. They are united, according to both perceptions, to both the twin natures of Christ, becoming one body with Him and fellow communicants of His glory and divinity. For it is thus that they are united to God who worthily, in knowledge and in contemplation, eat of this bread and drink of this cup with perceptive heart and soul. Those, however, who do this unworthily are empty of the Holy Spirit's gift. They nourish their bodies, but not their souls.

Conscious participation: an everlasting Pascha

Beloved, please do not make an uproar on hearing the truth made plain to you. For if you confess that the flesh of the Lord is bread which gives life to the world, and if you know His blood also gives life to those who partake of it, that it becomes in him who drinks it as a spring welling up into everlasting life, then how, tell me, do you in partaking of these not sense anything more added to your soul? Though you may probably feel a certain small joy, after a little while you are the same as you were before and feel in yourself no increase of life, or gushing spring, or see any light whatever. Because, while this looks like any fragment of bread to those who have not gone beyond the perception of their senses, yet, to the intellect, it is light uncontainable and unapproachable. So, too, is the wine in like manner light, life, fire, and living water. If therefore, on eating and drinking the bread and wine of gladness, you do not become aware that you live with an indestructible life, that the bread is in the form of light, or that you have received it like the prophet before [cf. Is 6:6-7] as a burning coal within you, that you have drunk the Master's blood as water which wells up and speaks within you, if you have in no way arrived at the contemplation of and participation in these things, how do you fancy that you have become a communicant of the life? How can you think that you have touched the unapproachable fire; or how do you suppose that you partake of eternal light? In no way at all has this happened to you, you who have no perception of these matters! Instead, the light shines on you who are blind; the fire warms you without touching you; the life overshadowed you but was not united with you; the living water passed through your soul like [ordinary] water through a pipe because it did not find in you a worthy receptacle. Therefore, while you are thus receiving and thus touching the untouchable and thinking that you eat, you remain without receiving, without eating, without having anything at all within yourself. For the unapproachable Word, the bread which comes down from heaven, is not held by the senses. Instead, it is He Himself Who comprehends and touches, and Who is united without confusion to all who are worthy and well prepared for His reception.

If, then, you celebrate the feast and so partake as well of the divine mysteries, all your life will be to you one single feast. And not a feast, but the beginning of a feast and a single Pascha, the passage and emigration from what is seen to what is sensed by the intellect, to that place where every shadow and type, and all the present symbols, come to an end, and where we who are pure shall in purity rejoice eternally in the most pure sacrifice, in God the Father and the co-essential Spirit, always seeing Christ and seen by Him, ever being with Christ, reigning with Christ, than Whom nothing is greater in the Kingdom of God, and to Whom is due all glory, honor and worship, together with the Father and His all-Holy and life-creating Spirit, now and ever, and unto ages of ages without end. Amen.

Index of Scriptural References

Index

Other Titles in the *Popular Patristics* Series from St Vladimir's Seminary Press:

St Ephrem the Syrian
Hymns on Paradise
(ISBN 0-88141-076-4)

St Isaac of Nineveh
On Ascetical Life
(ISBN 0-88141-077-2)

St Cyril of Jerusalem
On the Christian Sacraments
(ISBN 0-913836-39-7)

St John of Damascus
On the Divine Images
(ISBN 0-913836-62-1)

St Germanus of Constantinople
On the Divine Liturgy
(ISBN 0-88141-038-1)

St Theodore the Studite
On the Holy Icons
(ISBN 0-913836-76-1)

St Basil the Great
On the Holy Spirit
(ISBN 0-913836-74-5)

St John Chrysostom
On Marriage and Family Life
(ISBN 0-88141-86-9)

St Simeon the New Theologian
On the Mystical Life:
The Ethical Discourses
vol. 2: On Virtue and Christian Life
(ISBN 0-88141-143-4)
(forthcoming)
vol. 3: Life, Times and Theology
(ISBN 0-88141-144-2)
(forthcoming)

St John Chrysostom
On the Priesthood
(ISBN 0-913836-38-9)

St Gregory of Nyssa
On the Soul and Resurrection
(ISBN 0-88141-120-5)

St Cyril of Alexandria
On theUnity of Christ
(ISBN 0-88141-133-7)

St John Chrysostom
On Wealth and Poverty
(ISBN 0-88141-039-X)

To order any of the above titles, or to request our complete catalog of over 170 titles, call or write:

ST VLADIMIR'S SEMINARY PRESS
575 Scarsdale Road, Crestwood, NY 10707-1699
1-800-204-2665